Valuation

Leo Gough

FINANCE

05.07

- Fast track route to valuing companies and creating shareholder value

- Covers the key areas of valuation, from EVA and the importance of discounted cashflows to the disharmony in international accounting standards and valuing knowledge-based assets

- Examples and lessons from some of the world's most successful businesses, including News Corporation, Genentech and Nokia, and ideas from the smartest thinkers, including Warren Buffett, Baruch Lev, Joel Stern, Alfred Steinherr and Peter Drucker

- Includes a glossary of key concepts and a comprehensive resources guide

>>EXPRESS EXEC : COM<<
essential management thinking at your fingertips

First published 2002 by
Capstone Publishing (a Wiley company)
8 Newtec Place
Magdalen Road
Oxford OX4 1RE
United Kingdom
http://www.capstoneideas.com

CIP catalogue records for this book are available from the British Library and the US Library of Congress

ISBN 1-84112-335-8

Printed and bound in Great Britain

This book is printed on acid-free paper

Contents

Introduction to ExpressExec

ExpressExec is 3 million words of the latest management thinking compiled into 10 modules. Each module contains 10 individual titles forming a comprehensive resource of current business practice written by leading practitioners in their field. From brand management to balanced scorecard, ExpressExec enables you to grasp the key concepts behind each subject and implement the theory immediately. Each of the 100 titles is available in print and electronic formats.

Through the ExpressExec.com Website you will discover that you can access the complete resource in a number of ways:

» printed books or e-books;
» e-content – PDF or XML (for licensed syndication) adding value to an intranet or Internet site;
» a corporate e-learning/knowledge management solution providing a cost-effective platform for developing skills and sharing knowledge within an organization;
» bespoke delivery – tailored solutions to solve your need.

Why not visit www.expressexec.com and register for free key management briefings, a monthly newsletter and interactive skills checklists. Share your ideas about ExpressExec and your thoughts about business today.

Please contact elound@wiley-capstone.co.uk for more information.

Introduction

This chapter considers:

» shareholder value versus stakeholder claims;
» valuation measures such as cash flow and EVA.

"What is a cynic? A man who knows the price of everything, and the value of nothing."

Oscar Wilde, The Artist as Critic

The art of creating value is not just a discipline for accountants and investors. Used properly, it can be a powerful, perhaps *the* most powerful, way that managers can run their companies in an increasingly competitive world. By integrating accounting and performance measures with strategic thinking and day-to-day operations, managers can learn to take decisions that enhance their businesses and add real value.

Most managers agree that value creation is important – but how do you measure it? As knowledge capital becomes increasingly important, traditional financial measures such as earnings and book value are accounting for less and less of a company's actual market price. Investors are paying great attention to non-financial factors in their efforts to assess the value of corporations. This should be welcome news to managers, who are well aware of the value of "intangibles" such as R&D, patents, trademarks, copyrights, brand names, employee talent, distribution channels, new ideas and processes. A well-known example of a great value-creating idea is Wal-Mart's system that gives its suppliers direct access to its inventory. A customer buys an item at Wal-Mart and the barcode information goes directly to Procter & Gamble, who maintains the inventory. It's a huge gain in efficiency that gives Wal-Mart the edge over its competitors.

In the USA, the importance of "shareholder value" is almost universally accepted in business. The concept is here defined as being not only the "market value added" (MVA) – this is the difference between the stock market capitalization of a company and the capital that has been invested in it – but also growth in employment and high productivity. Although share prices fluctuate, over time they tend to reflect the underlying value of a company.

Above all else, American CEOs and senior managers are expected to focus on creating shareholder value in their corporations. Not so in Europe and Asia. In these regions, corporations are seen as having other obligations to their communities. Governments often overtly define and regulate a company's duties towards its "stakeholders" (employees, customers, suppliers, the state, lenders, investors and the general public). Critics condemn the shareholder value approach as harmful to society as a whole, and the rights and obligations of stakeholders are given greater weight.

Supporters of the stakeholder system have argued that focusing on shareholder value may hurt the interests of other stakeholders, in particular the employees of the company. The counter-argument is that the most successful companies in any given market will tend to enjoy better productivity, better MVA, and employ more people than their competitors. In other words, successful companies are maximizing shareholder value even if they do not explicitly say so. In doing so they are also benefiting, not damaging, the other stakeholders' interests.

Shareholder value implies a stock market where company shares are widely held by the public. Company information is less easily available in countries such as Germany and Japan, where shareholdings are concentrated in the hands of institutions. Share prices may not reflect values as closely as they do in more efficient stock markets. There is less incentive for managers to strive to create shareholder value.

Furthermore, the specter of a hostile takeover does not loom as powerfully as it does in the USA. The USA has a vigorous market for mergers and acquisitions (M&A) that is partly driven by perceived weaknesses in the current management. Elsewhere, managers may not be as concerned that inefficiency may lead to a takeover.

Despite these philosophical differences, Europe and Asia are seeking to become more efficient. M&A activity has blossomed and deregulation is the order of the day. Many companies are recognizing the benefits of having a measurement that incorporates all known information and allows managers to see the effects of good decisions reflected in their company's share price. Others, however, believe that too great a focus on a single measure for shareholder value encourages short termism, which can ultimately be value destroying (see Chapter 6). To the extent that the stakeholder approach encourages good long-term relationships along the supply chain, between the company and its workforce and with customers, this philosophy may indeed create value over time, but adding value is not the primary goal of the stakeholder concept.

Adding value is done by concentrating on increasing cash flows to shareholders in the form of dividends and share price appreciation. It is these cash flows, rather than accounting earnings, that are the most important indicator of value creation/destruction. Creating value is not short-termist. Nor is it vague. MVA and its relative, EVA (Economic Value Added), which is the profit earned after deducting the cost of capital invested, are eminently measurable. Approaches such as Value Based Management (VBM) are being widely used to focus the entire organization on creating value.

From an investor's perspective, a company must generate returns that not only allow it to stay in business but also give its investors an adequate reward for their investment. Hard-nosed investors compare returns across companies, industries and countries over time. They will move their capital from poorly performing companies to better ones and away from countries that they perceive as investor-unfriendly. Unless a government bails it out, a company that investors consistently avoid will lack capital. Its market value will decrease to the level at which it does generate an acceptable return. This is damaging to all stakeholders in the firm – everybody loses. The challenge for managers is to earn more than the cost of capital over the long term, thereby creating value.

This material will explore how these ideas are applied in practice and show why so many major companies have adopted this approach, including Coca Cola, Westinghouse, Siemens and Tate & Lyle. The commercialization of the Internet and the "New Economy" frenzy has caused some people to doubt the relevance of existing valuation methods to e-business. This is essentially because people are experimenting with unproven business models, some of which will fail.

As these new industries begin to mature and produce financial returns it will become clear that the long-term winners do what all winning companies do: create value.

What is Valuation?

This chapter examines the following concepts related to valuation:
» who needs to know the value? – lenders, investors and managers;
» objections to EPS and PE as measures;
» rate-of-return measures;
» discounted cash flow;
» intangibles;
» EVA and other proprietary measures.

"Earnings per share tells nothing about the cost of generating those profits ..."

Peter Keen, prominent IT consultant

Three main groups need to know the value of a business: the owners, the lenders and the managers. Their interests do not necessarily coincide. According to Joel Stern, who coined the term "EVA" in 1972 and is a leading exponent of shareholder value, modern accounting practice grew out of the need of investors and lenders to prevent managers from misusing company funds. In the 1920s and 30s, for instance, it was not uncommon in corporate America for managers to "self-deal", that is, to purchase from suppliers that they secretly owned personally. Furthermore, there were potential conflicts between lenders and investors. How could a lender be sure that managers were not paying out excessively high dividends to their shareholders, or undertaking very risky enterprises?

Joel Zimmerman, a professor of accounting at the Simon School of Business, points out that modern accounting practice developed as a compromise that managers made with lenders. The managers would hire respectable third-party accountants to monitor their business and report to lenders.

That is the problem, say value enthusiasts. They point out that lenders are not interested in businesses as a going concern, since they have little or nothing to gain. Lenders want to know the liquidation value of a company, to judge their chances of recovering their loan should the company fail. Accountancy has developed over the last century to do this kind of conservative reporting job very well, but it does not provide good ways of valuing a healthy business from an investor's viewpoint.

THE CHALLENGE FOR SENIOR EXECUTIVES

The senior managers of large public companies rarely have very large shareholdings in their companies. This separation between ownership and management has existed for most of the twentieth century, but the communication between the two groups is less than perfect. Under pressure from institutional investors, executives may find it necessary to "manage" earnings to satisfy fashions in performance measurement.

In 1998 the Securities and Exchange Commission chairman, Arthur Levitt, attacked a number of widespread accounting practices that distort the true picture of company results. In the following year, the well-known investor Warren Buffett supported Levitt's remarks and said in Berkshire Hathaway's annual report that "a significant and growing number of otherwise high-grade managers – CEOs you would be happy to have as spouses for your children or trustees under your will – have come to the view that it is okay to manipulate earnings to satisfy what they believe are Wall Street's desires. Indeed, many CEOs think this kind of manipulation is not only okay, but actually their *duty*."

EARNINGS PER SHARE (EPS) AND PRICE/EARNINGS (PE)

For many years EPS has been the principal measure used to evaluate performance. EPS is simply the net income of a company divided by the number of shares in issue. In the short term it can be artificially manipulated by, for example, temporarily slashing budgets such as advertising. Furthermore, argue critics, EPS tend to understate the real value of a company in many industries because of the GAAP (Generally Accepted Accounting Principles) view that items such as R&D and training should be treated as expenses in the year in which they occur. In industries where these items are a major expenditure and have a long-term effect, such as high tech (R&D) and financial services (training), EPS critics say that it would be more realistic to treat them as capital expenditure and amortize them over a number of years.

Based on EPS, the price/earnings ratio (PE), which is the ratio of the share price to earnings per share, has been used as a way of valuing stocks. Investors ask themselves how much they have to pay to invest in a company with a given level of earnings, and the PE provides the answer. A high PE indicates that the company's market value is high – and is therefore expensive – or, according to another interpretation, that expectations of future growth are high. Over the last half century average PEs have generally fluctuated between 10 and 20, but when an industry booms PEs can shoot up to stratospheric levels, suggesting that the market expects earnings to grow rapidly in the future.

The assumption has been that EPS growth is mirrored by a growth in a company's share price. Some studies of the US and other markets have not found this to be the case in practice – there is little or no correlation, overall, between EPS growth and PE growth, at least in the short to medium term.

Clearly this is unsatisfactory. We want to know what a company is worth and, if we are investors, we can judge the value of our investment by the cash we can obtain by selling our shares. Positive EPS growth does not tell us that the share price will go up. Something is wrong with this picture.

In practice, buyers of shares don't only look at earnings figures when deciding how much they are willing to pay in the market. They also consider many other kinds of information relating to the possible future earnings of a company. Much of this is "soft" data. Investors ask themselves questions such as: "Do I believe that Product X is so great that its market share will grow from 5% to 60% in three years? My daughter likes it." Product X may change the fortunes of a company, but by the time this shows up in the EPS the share price may have already risen in response. For new investors, it will be too late.

RATE OF RETURN

Recognizing the shortcomings of EPS as a measure, some people have turned to rate-of-return calculations such as ROE (return on equity), ROCE (return on capital employed), ROI (return on investment) and RONA (return on net assets) in the search for a better way to value companies. These measures have been widely used as performance indicators for senior management, especially in the US. There is evidence of some correlation between ROCE/ROE growth and growth in share prices, but at an unacceptably low level.

Rate-of-return measures are just as easy to manipulate as EPS. Eager for bonuses, management may shun good business opportunities or reduce the equity in their firm to make the figures look better. Executives who are compensated using RONA may avoid highly profitable acquisitions because the increased asset base will reduce the RONA figure and hence their bonuses. Conversely, it is tempting to sell valuable assets cheaply if the sale does not proportionately lower profitability. In the case of ROE, a trend of improving performance improves the figures – but so does buying back shares from the public, even if the company has to borrow the money, so long as the profit level remains constant.

EXECUTIVE COMPENSATION AND RATE-OF-RETURN MEASURES

Warren Buffett, one of the world's most successful investors, says:

> "I do not mind paying a manager a lot of money for good performance but I am bothered by mediocre managers getting large sums of money. Unfortunately the system feeds on itself and there is not much that you can do to correct this problem."[1]

DISCOUNTED CASH FLOW (DCF)

"Investing is the art of putting in cash now to get more cash later on," says Warren Buffett. The technique of DCF is to estimate all future free cash flows that a business is expected to generate, to discount them to their present value, and then to add all the figures together. Why discount future cash flows? Consider the following: is $1,000 that you expect to earn in five years' time as valuable as $1,000 that you will receive tomorrow? Clearly not, since you could invest tomorrow's $1,000 and earn interest on it for five years. To calculate today's value of $1,000 earned in five years' time, you "discount" it, by reducing at a given annual percentage rate. Not everyone uses the same percentage. Buffett, for instance, uses the US Treasury rate for long-term bonds, while others use higher rates.

Calculating future cash flows is naturally an exercise in forecasting. It can never produce a precisely accurate figure and when interest rates move or a company revises its forecasts of future cash flows, the numbers will change. Forecasting future cash flows is particularly difficult in rapidly developing industries, such as e-commerce. See Chapter 8 for an explanation of how to calculate DCF.

INTANGIBLES

One of the reasons why future cash flows are hard to estimate is the difficulty of measuring "intangibles." These, as we saw in Chapter 1, are valuable knowledge assets such as patents, brands, copyrights, and employee talents and know-how. In high-tech industries such as medical biotechnology, a successful product may ultimately be worth billions but only if it passes the rigorous Food and Drug Administration's trials, which take years to complete.

GENOMICS: ADDING VALUE THROUGH KNOWLEDGE

In mid-2000, the fledgling genomics industry (a subset of biotechnology) had grown in market value from $13bn in the previous year to $70bn, largely because of the successful mapping of the human genome and a huge increase in discovery rates. Says Edwin Kania, a venture capitalist at AGTC Funds in Boston:

"One of the things that we think will define the next wave of this industry is that a base knowledge has been set ... the 'Lego blocks' have been defined to the extent that engineers and inventors will now begin to try to understand what they can do that's useful with those building blocks."[2]

With so much potential for adding value, the search for good metrics for intangibles is gathering pace. Baruch Lev, a professor of accounting and finance at New York University's Stern School of Business, has been campaigning for greater public disclosure of information affecting intangibles. In an interview in 2001, Lev said:

"I just started working with two major companies, one a pharmaceutical company and the other a chemical company. I'm specifically tracing their knowledge capital and knowledge earnings to the drivers, which are investments in intangibles like R&D, advertising and information technology. The main thing these companies are interested in is how tracking and disclosing more information on their intangibles can benefit their business strategy ... I see clear signs from capital markets that people are realizing that these [intangibles] are, by far, the most important assets and that they need more information."

ECONOMIC VALUE ADDED (EVA) AND OTHER NEW PROPRIETARY MEASURES

Based on the concept of shareholder value, the definition of EVA is net operating profit after tax (NOPAT) minus a charge representing the company's cost of capital.

EXAMPLE 2.1: CALCULATING EVA

Company X has capital of $10mn and a cost of capital of 10%.
This year its NOPAT figure is $2.5mn.
Cost of capital @ 10% = $1mn.
EVA = $2.5mn − $1mn = $1.5mn

EVA experts make numerous adjustments to the accounting NOPAT figure to reflect the issues discussed earlier in this chapter, such as treating R&D and training as an investment rather than an expense. Similarly, the cost of capital often includes the after-tax cost of borrowing, long-term interest rates on government bonds, a risk premium, and a "blending" to reflect the proportions of debt and equity in the company. Joel Stern, of Stern Stewart, the original authors of EVA, estimates that the cost of capital was 10–13% in 2000.

EVA demands that companies make more than their cost of capital. If they don't, they are destroying value. In large companies, the sheer complexities of accounting and the reporting requirements of stock market regulators can cause executives to lose sight of this. EVA gets back to the basic question, "are we really making money?"

As a metric for executive performance, it aligns the interests of managers and shareholders. Most EVA companies use the measure not only for the company as a whole, but also for each division and sometimes every unit, outlet and product line, which leads to better decisions at every level.

Although EVA is the most widely accepted new approach to valuation, other consultants with similar proprietary concepts are competing for executives' attention, including those shown in Table 2.1.

These approaches are all attempts to measure and improve managers' contribution to value.

Table 2.1

Concept	Consultancy
TBR (total business return)	Boston Consulting Group
CFROI (cash flow return on investment)	Holt
Economic profit	McKinsey
SVA (shareholder value added)	LEK/Alcar

KEY POINTS

» Increasingly, executives and investors are becoming dissatisfied with conventional accounting figures as valuation measures.

» EPS and PE have been the financial community's main way of judging performance, on the assumption that EPS growth will lead to an increase in share price. Since EPS figures can be distorted, this does not generally occur in practice.

» Some firms use rate-of-return measures to judge performance. These figures can also be distorted, however, and can lead to value-destroying management decisions.

» Many investors and companies use discounted cash flow to value businesses. This approach works best in well-established industries where income is relatively predictable.

» With "knowledge assets" growing ever more important, a broadly based campaign has developed to find ways of measuring these "intangibles."

» EVA measures after-tax profit less the cost of capital. It encourages firms to focus on the creation of true shareholder value.

NOTES

1 Quoted in "The Return of the Buffetteers," by John Price, Investor Journal, the magazine of *Investors Alliance*, August 1998.

2 Gough, L. (2001) *Investing in Biotechnology Stocks*, John Wiley, Singapore.

The Evolution of Valuation

Accounting and valuation methods have developed as business has evolved. This chapter looks at:

- » the need for accounting reform;
- » Benjamin Graham, the father of stock analysis;
- » value investing today – Warren Buffett;
- » CAPM;
- » assessing risk;
- » derivatives.

Maybe I have just been in this business too long, and have seen too many global visions come and go. In 1979 everyone knew that it was a Malthusian world, that the energy crisis was just the beginning of a global struggle for ever-scarcer resources. In 1989 everyone knew that the big story was the struggle for the key manufacturing sectors, and that the winners would be those countries with coherent top-down industrial policies, whose companies weren't subject to the short-term pressures of financial markets. And in 1999 everybody knows that it's a global knowledge economy, where only those countries that tear down their walls, and open themselves to the winds of electronic commerce, will succeed. I wonder what everybody will know in 2009?

Paul Krugman, economist[1]

Although accounting in commerce has existed for literally thousands of years, it was not until the 1400s that double-entry bookkeeping was devised. Renaissance Italy raised commerce to new levels of sophistication, empowered by such factors as widespread literacy, stable private property laws, the availability of capital and credit, and an efficient numerical system. The Franciscan friar Luca Pacioli, a mathematician and friend of Leonardo da Vinci, popularized the double-entry system in a book published in 1494. This event is widely seen as being the major landmark in the development of modern accounting. Pacioli's system is recognizably the forerunner of today's accounting methods, tailored to the needs of a fifteenth-century merchant. Three things were essential in business, Pacioli declared: enough cash or credit, good bookkeeping, and a system of accounts that enables merchants to assess their finances rapidly.

Accounting and valuation methods evolve to meet the needs of commerce. As business organizations have grown larger and more complex, new and more sophisticated techniques have been devised. The concept of the joint stock company, the development of formalized stock markets, improved banking and regulatory oversight have all played major roles in creating the system that exists today.

As mentioned in Chapter 2, modern accounting developed to protect lenders and investors from the potential for managerial abuse. In the US in the late 1800s industrial growth was enormous, but brought with it numerous scandals and financial panics as the country moved from an agricultural to an industrialized economy. Concerns over monopolistic power and the exploitation of workers brought about anti-trust legislation and the labor unions that we still have today. Teddy Roosevelt, becoming president in 1901, was a key figure in increasing government regulation of large industries, widening the Interstate Commerce Commission's powers. The ICC established a uniform system of accounting and a new player entered the lender/investor/manager circle – the government itself. For the first time, a government used accounting as a way of regulating industry.

Until the 1920s, US balance sheets were intended mainly for lenders who were primarily concerned about liquidity, not earnings potential, but when wholesale prices began to fall drastically as a result of overproduction, companies began to look for investors who were less interested in current cash flow. Issuing shares on the stock market became the most attractive way to raise funds, and accounting began to emphasize revenue and expenses over the balance sheet.

The "roaring twenties" culminated in a stock market boom. By 1929, news of the stock market had come to dominate popular culture. Practices that are criminalized today, such as insider trading, were common and accepted. Small investors were able to borrow heavily from brokers in order to speculate. In September 1929, for instance, brokers' loans grew by $670mn. In October, the famous Wall Street Crash began. According to the economist J.K. Galbraith, the search for the catalyst of the crash is useless – "it is in the nature of a speculative boom that almost anything can collapse it."[2]

Despite attempts by leading financial figures to talk up the market, by November 1929 it was clear that something was seriously wrong; stocks had dropped by 50% in a matter of weeks. Margin calls wiped out private investors and ruined the heavily leveraged investment trusts of the time. Government intervention only made matters worse, and by 1932 competitive currency devaluations around the world had brought about a worldwide economic depression, a disaster that the accounting and banking systems of the day had signally failed to predict or prevent. Quite simply, people had not been able to assess values.

BENJAMIN GRAHAM

Widely regarded as the father of stock market analysis, Benjamin Graham was a fund manager who was wiped out in the 1929 crash. In 1934 he published *Security Analysis*,[3] a formidable tome that is one of the key books to establish an intellectual framework for the objective valuation of public companies. Graham was not concerned with the actual businesses of the companies he studied – their products, services and market potential were, he felt, too difficult to measure. Instead, he focused on identifying companies that had a low share price relative to their asset value.

Graham turned stock market analysis from an art into an organized discipline, if not a science. One of the first people to actually study published records, he was able to explode many fondly held invest-ment illusions of the time. His approach was strictly quantitative – for Graham, figures were the only things that mattered when assessing a company.

One of Graham's innovations that has become a standard measure is the comparison of a company's historical rate of return with that of high grade bonds over the same period. Suppose that over a 10-year period bonds yield a 4% average annual return and a given stock yields 9%. The yield gap between the two is 5%, which Graham regarded as an acceptable "margin of safety" for an investor. Graham wrote at length about the doubtful accuracy of company accounts – the margin of safety idea was principally to protect investors from losses due to poor accounting practices.

As an investor, Graham's greatest strength was in just saying no. After experimentation with many complex forms of analysis, he concluded that the safest method for the non-professional was only to invest in what he termed "bargain issues," which are companies whose share price are currently less than their net current assets (that is, ignoring the value of their fixed assets entirely). The number of bargain issues available at any particular time varies with the mood of the stock market – if there are many available, then the market is depressed.

Graham was not a great believer in "growth stocks," those compa-nies that are expected to rise and rise for many years. He argued that it is extremely difficult to identify such a company correctly, and that most analysts and fund managers are usually wrong in their assessments, tending to buy growth stocks either long after they have matured into slow growth or as speculations that never deliver on their promise.

Graham was successful as an investor by concentrating almost exclusively on grossly undervalued situations. A Grahamite stock market portfolio was generally a sorry sight, being a collection of "cigar butts" with one or two puffs left – unpopular, unpromising low-cap companies that look unappetizing to the average investor. His point was that these firms, selected by stringent criteria, are likely to be severely underpriced and at some point in the future the market will recognize this and bid them up to their fair value, at which point the Grahamite investor must sell.

As was discussed in Chapter 2, earnings per share and price/earnings ratios are falling out of favor as measures. Graham was devoted to them. One of his principal criteria for investment was that the earnings yield on a stock, which is the inverse of the p/e ratio, should be double the current AAA bond yield.[4]

VALUE INVESTING TODAY

Graham's most famous disciple is Warren Buffett, one of the world's wealthiest men. Buffett started out by following his mentor's methods, but by the 1960s he had become increasingly interested in the future potential of the businesses he studied – merely seeking out undervalued "bargain issues" was not enough. In 1963 American Express was the victim of a salad oil fraud that left it potentially liable for $150mn. Amex was not a company Graham would have considered, with few tangible assets. Buffet decided it was a "franchise" company, meaning that it had a virtual monopoly of its market, and loaded up on the stock despite the risk from the salad oil liability, and was richly rewarded. Two years later he did the same with Disney, judging that its fictional characters and film library amounted to a franchise. In recognizing the potential value of intellectual assets and brands, Buffett was indeed ahead of his time. By the 1990s Buffett was worth over $10bn, all held with his fund, Berkshire Hathaway, which is a major shareholder of such un-Grahamite stocks as Coca Cola and Amex. He has also bought many smaller companies outright. Like his mentor, Buffett takes no interest in the ups and downs of the market and does not believe that anyone can predict them accurately. He invests for the very long term, confident that the market will eventually recognize the true value of a great business.

CAPM

Since the 1960s, many models have been proposed for estimating the cost of capital – and the relative risk – for a specific company. The most durable of these is the Capital Asset Pricing Model, or CAPM.

CAPM assumes that investors want a minimum rate of return even if there is no risk, and that they raise this rate as the perceived risk increases. CAPM uses three inputs in its formula.

1 The risk-free rate, which is taken to be the current rate on government bonds.
2 The average rate of return on the equity market over a given time period when valuations have been "normal" (i.e. not too high or too low).
3 The beta – this figure represents the relative risk of a given company compared with the risk of the market overall. It attempts to measure how the stock price has moved in unison with the overall market. Taking the beta of the overall market as 1, companies usually have betas that range from 0.5 to 1.5. Beta predicts share price volatility – a company with a beta of 0.5 is, in theory, less volatile than the market and will rise and fall less sharply than the market overall.

In recent years, critics of CAPM have gathered strength. According to CAPM if you invest in a diversified set of stocks whose beta is 0, the same value as a "risk-free" investment such as a bank deposit, you should obtain similar returns. Studies have shown that portfolios with a beta of 0 have done better than predicted by CAPM over the long term. Furthermore, in the 1980s US mutual funds produced results that bore no relation to their betas and the betas of many companies fluctuate over time. Doubts have been expressed over whether you can really measure overall stock market performance accurately. Using different market indices to represent the overall market produces widely different beta values for individual stocks.

ASSESSING RISK

One of the most important developments in finance during the twentieth century is an increasingly sophisticated understanding of risk. It is still a young science and, as we shall see below, many large companies have made terrible blunders in recent years through the misuse of newer risk management techniques.

To investors, it is a disturbing thought that if you could have invested a relatively small sum, say $100,000, for a 5% annual real return at the time of Jesus Christ, it would now be worth more than the entire world's GDP. This could not be done because in the very long term whole economic systems have been disrupted by war and other disasters, and investments have become worthless. The thought should disturb managers too. Nothing, certainly not companies or financial assets, are permanent stores of value.

We like to ignore this uncomfortable notion in our daily lives, but students of risk insist that it is relevant. Companies do not have total control over their destinies – and they can be damaged by many less dramatic risks than the specter of a total economic collapse. We like to believe that high growth is never-ending, but the truth may well be that it is out of our hands.

One striking 1986 study by William Baumol, an economist at Princeton, looked at long-term productivity rates in 72 countries from 1870 to 1980.[5] The least productive countries in 1870 had the highest productivity increases in the succeeding years, while the most productive countries had the slowest growth. Overall, countries' productivity have tended to converge, moving from a range of 8:1 to 2:1, despite very different economic systems and policies. As long as our present system remains stable, we can expect a regression to the mean average as technology and education spread across the globe. Regression to the mean is not a safe way to predict the long-term future, however, because of periodic discontinuities. Like our hypothetical investor 2000 years ago, we have no way of knowing what will happen in the far future.

Both investors and managers would like to have certainty where there is none available, and many useful theories have been distorted in their application in order to satisfy people's need for confidence. CAPM's focus on volatility led many to equate stock price volatility with risk, but they are not the same thing. More recent work has concentrated on the idea that high returns are intimately associated with high risk. In general, companies and investors seeking abnormally high returns must expect greater dangers.

An identical proposition carries a different risk level depending on who you are. Wealthy organizations can take bigger risks with a small part of their wealth because they can absorb losses. An individual with profound knowledge of a situation may be in a better position to judge a risk than an outsider. Risks are often very hard to measure – you may know something is risky, but you don't know exactly how risky it is. Furthermore, individuals and organizations do not always behave rationally. Since the 1970s, interesting work has been done on the irrationality of decision-making that overturned previous theories which assumed that everyone took decisions rationally, based on their own best interests.

Prospect Theory is an important contribution to the psychological aspect of risk and decision-taking. Developed by psychologists Daniel Kahneman and Amos Tversky,[6] Prospect Theory examines the ways that people are affected by their emotions and also make intellectual errors when making choices. Much depends on how the problem is depicted. For example, lung cancer patients at a certain hospital had a shorter life expectancy if they received radiation therapy than if they opted for surgery, but a few patients died on the operating table. The overall difference in life expectancy was not great and it was difficult to choose which therapy to accept. When patients were presented with the options in terms of the risk of death under surgery, nearly half opted for radiation therapy. Patients who were given the same choice expressed in terms of life expectancy, only a fifth chose radiation therapy. No facts were hidden: they were simply presented in a different light.

DERIVATIVES

Human error has an enormous effect on the values of companies, and it is much more subtle that simply making a mistake in calculation. We can be blind to risks. One good example in recent years is in derivatives. These immensely complex financial instruments are generally designed to reduce risk and came into their own following the publication of the Black-Scholes model for pricing financial options and the subsequent rapid growth of financial futures markets. Many huge and highly respected firms bought and sold packages of derivatives as a hedge against the various risks in their businesses, much to the benefit of the financial institutions who sold them and often acted as counter-parties to the risk. In the past few years, there have been a number of celebrated disasters in which blue chip firms in the US and Europe, such as Metallgesellschaft and Procter & Gamble, and even regional governments have suffered massive losses from the use of these instruments that were designed to reduce risk.

Derivatives *can* be used to reduce risk, but only if you are very careful about your assumptions. The problem was that the finance departments of various organizations came to be seen as profit centers – by using derivatives, you could make large profits though leverage, assuming you accepted or ignored the risks that went with it. Procter & Gamble, for example, took on a derivatives deal in 1993 on the assumption that short-term interest rates would continue to fall as they had done for several years. In the following year interest rates rose and Procter & Gamble was in serious trouble. Like others who got into trouble, the predictable response was a flurry of lawsuits in an attempt to avoid liability.

More recently, a celebrated hedge fund, Long Term Capital Management (LTCM), that boasted two Nobel Prize winning economists among its partners, lost $2bn in a single year by betting the wrong way on global interest rates. Mark Mobius, the emerging markets investor, has this to say about the derivatives scene:

> "so-called derivatives ... are not fully understood by the participants ... they're making all kinds of assumptions that are very tenuous ... they'll mistake the difference between causation and correlation. They'll say, 'every time the coffee is hot, the market goes up; therefore I'll buy a derivative for hot coffee ...'"[7]

KEY INSIGHTS

» The financial system develops in response to the changing needs of business. The system focuses on maintaining stability, without which values can collapse entirely.

» Value is not the same as growth. From the investor's point of view, buying stocks that are cheaper than their intrinsic value may be wiser than investing in dynamic but overpriced companies.

» The greatest progress in financial theory in the last century has probably been the development of a better understanding of risk. Risk management raises your chances of making acceptable returns without having to make accurate predictions about the future.

NOTES

1 "Understanding Globalization," a book review in *The Washington Monthly*, June 1999, Vol. 31, Issue 6.

2 Galbraith, J.K. (1961) *The Great Crash: 1929*, Houghton Mifflin.

3 Graham, B. (1934) *Security Analysis*, New York: McGraw-Hill.

4 "Triple A" bonds, the top-rated bonds in Standard & Poor's rating system, are considered virtually free of the risk of default.

5 Baumol, W. (1986) "Productivity Growth, Convergence and Welfare: What the Long-run Show," *American Economic Review*, 76, 1072–85.

6 For more information on Prospect Theory, see: Kahneman, D., Slovic, P. and Tversky, A. (eds.) (1982) *Judgement under Uncertainty: Heuristics and Biases*, Cambridge University Press, Cambridge; Kahneman, D. and Tversky, A. (1973) "On the psychology of prediction," *Psychological Review*, 80, 237–51; and Kahneman, D. and Tversky, A. (1979) "Prospect theory: An analysis of decision under risk," *Econometrica*, 263–91.

7 Gough, L. (1999) *Trading the World's Markets*, John Wiley, Singapore.

The E-Dimension

The problems with valuation of the dotcoms are well known – but what is the solution? This chapter discusses:

» tall e-stories;
» EVA online;
» cannibalizing existing businesses.

"If I taught a course on company evaluation, I would ask the following question in the exam: Evaluate the following internet company ... Anyone who gave an answer would be flunked."

Charlie Munger, vice chairman of Berkshire Hathaway, the investment vehicle of the legendary investor Warren Buffett

It is quite rare to witness a speculative boom of world-shaking proportions, yet that is what we have just experienced in the commercialization of the Internet at the turn of the century. The study of booms reveals much about valuation, since they are the exceptions that prove the rule. Common sense and experience are ignored as people eagerly develop new theories to explain how some firms have suddenly become staggeringly rich.

The dotcom boom is little different from earlier speculative frenzies. The nineteenth-century railway craze, the auto and aviation booms of the early twentieth century and the tech boom of the 1960s are just a few examples of periods when almost everyone involved – investors, lenders, managers and legislators – seemed to take leave of their senses. Such booms are usually based on the introduction of a new resource or technology that is of real value. This is clearly true of the Internet, which, at the very least, is a tremendous gain in the speed and efficiency of communications. Even genuine benefits can be overvalued, however; the Great Western Railway was the most popular railway company in Britain in the nineteenth century, but if you had bought shares at its launch in 1835 and held them until 1913, you would have gained an annual return of only 5%.

Speaking in 1998 Marc Faber, a veteran fund manager based in the Far East, remarked that Internet stocks

"have a much higher valuation than anything I've seen before in terms of price to earnings, price to sales and so forth ... As a group, maybe they have topped out already. Now they're buying each other. The new issue calendar is now mainly internet stocks. When the new issue calendar was just oil servicing stocks in the 1980s, it was very close to the end... I think the writing is really on the wall."[1]

Not many people were listening to such "old-fashioned" views then, but as stock prices continued to rise so did the professionals' qualms. Andrew Klein, founder of WitCapital (now WitSoundView), was the first person to successfully complete a public offering of shares on the Internet. In early 2000 Klein spoke for many when he said that there was clearly

> "a gap between what the market is willing to pay and what educated, sophisticated investors would predict to be sustainable values over the near term ... in hindsight, [some of] those valuations may look justified. There will be others that crash and burn and therefore their valuations will look very foolish. That's the hard part – it's very hard to tell which is which at this point."[2]

When the market goes mad ...

"The fate of the world economy is now totally dependent on the US stock market, whose growth is dependent on about 50 stocks, half of which have never reported any earnings."
Paul Volcker, ex-chairman of the US Federal Reserve,
September, 1999

The year 2000 saw a horrific crash in the stock prices of Internet firms. According to Salomon Smith Barney's estimates, between January 14, 2000, and March 22, 2001, about $4.7trn worth of wealth simply vanished from US stock exchanges. Many well-known Internet stocks dropped in value by 80% or more from their highs, including eBay (down 72%), Amazon (down 77%), Yahoo! (down 84%), and CNet (down 72%), while hundreds of lesser names simply went out of business.

Railways, automobiles and flight brought huge economic benefits long after share prices crashed – and the same is likely to be true for the Internet, but exactly how this could happen will only be known in hindsight. Even during the boom there was a demand for a justification of the high valuations of what were mostly unprofitable companies, and an abundance of gurus appeared to theorize about the "New Economy."

This is not to suggest that anyone making a positive remark in a bull market is foolish or disingenuous. Information technology (IT) needs to be explained – in time, the e-revolution may come to be seen as an integral part of a massive long-term IT revolution rather than as a distinct phenomenon. Companies must adopt new technologies; employees, legislators, and the public must be educated; and investors must be wooed. Internet apostles often exceeded the limits of their spheres of competence, however, by making naïve claims. Here are just three examples.

TALL E-STORIES

1 "It's not the product that matters. We will create long term customer relationships and sell a huge range of products and services to them."

   Consumers are not only capricious; they are also intolerant of transparent ploys. There are very few, if any, Internet companies that have significantly widened their range successfully yet.

2 "Our aim is to create a worldwide brand. We focus on rapid growth now, not profits. Once we dominate our market, we will control prices and make huge profits."

   A few internet companies, such as Yahoo!, Amazon, and eBay have indeed become household names, but monopolistic pricing and large profits look improbable at present.

3 "We can turn eyeballs, page views, click-throughs, etc. into revenue for our company."

   With the exception of Yahoo!, selling Internet advertising has not been a sustainable way of generating income, because online advertising has been largely ineffective.

CASE STUDY: VALUING YAHOO!

Here's how an Internet analyst at a major investment bank (he prefers not to be named) perceived Yahoo!'s valuation in early 2000.

As the company's income grows, its PE will decline to a less surprising level. Since the mid-90s, Yahoo!'s income has grown 100% year-on-year. The way to value Yahoo! is to look at its increasing share of US advertising expenditure overall. In 1996, the total US advertising spend was $120bn. In 1998, it had grown slightly to $125bn. In 1996, the total online advertising spend was $314mn, but by 1998, it had grown to $2.1bn. During the same period, Yahoo!'s market share of online advertising grew from 10% to 25%; it earned $800mn in 1998. They are generating 400 million page views a day, so they clearly have the wind at their backs. By 2002/3, Yahoo! could have a 50% market share of online advertising.

From 1996-99, Yahoo! had gross margins of 85% - its cost of sales is low. Its operating margins have been growing, from 35% in 1996 to around 40% now (early 2000). Most of the difference has been spent on sales and marketing, but this figure will decline now that more people are aware of the brand.

Assume that Yahoo! achieves a 50% operating margin in 2002/3, and has 50% of the online advertising market. The midpoint of estimates of the total online advertising spend in 2002/3 is $20bn (estimates have been as high as $44bn). In this scenario, Yahoo!'s 2002/3 revenue will be $10bn, with an operating margin of 50%, or $5bn. Currently the market capitalization of Yahoo! is around $100bn, so you are only paying 20 times the potential 2002/3 revenue. That's cheaper than many old-line companies.

Yahoo!'s stock price peaked at $250 in 2000. In late July 2001, it had dropped to $17.42, reducing its market capitalization to $9761bn, less than a tenth of the figure quoted in the preceding paragraph ($100bn). The company's sales grew at a stunning rate between fiscal years 1995 ($1.4mn) and 2000 ($1110.2mn). In the last quarter of 2000, however, the company showed a loss ($97.8mn). Losses continued during the first two quarters of 2001 ($11.5mn and $48.5mn respectively), with sales dropping by more than a third.

Safa Rashtchy, an analyst at PiperJaffray, commented in July 2001 that:

> The problem, of course, is that the demand for online advertising has slowed considerably ... The business model of Yahoo! is changing as they realize that even with a

rebound in online advertising, they still need to make money through other ways, primarily through fee-based services or subscriptions, for them to sustain the growth that they have had.

If you look at the traditional publishers, they always have two components to their revenue: subscription and advertising. That hasn't been the case in online advertising because there was so much revenue coming from advertising and so much free content available that nobody thought about charging people. And now Yahoo! and other companies are beginning to think that they have to make money in a number of ways, much like the offline people.

Although *The Economist* magazine estimates that the online advertising spend is estimated to drop radically to $9bn in the US in 2001, Yahoo! is, in many ways, a success story. One of the few Internet companies to have both built a brand and made profits, it stands out among the casualties of the dotcom bust, and may ultimately achieve its aims – at which point it will become easier to value. Today most conservative investors would regard it as a risky investment.

As we have seen, the movement to find better ways of evaluating knowledge capital is growing fast. In the case of the dotcoms, it did not develop quickly enough. Donna Hoffman, a professor of management at Vanderbilt University, is a dedicated campaigner for a rational approach to commercializing the Internet. Voted by *Newsweek* as one of the "50 people who matter most on the internet," Professor Hoffman has served as an expert witness in a number of celebrated Internet court cases, and has been a forceful advocate of improving the measurement of Internet use. She argues that companies were often misguided in their approach.

"The most important factor in the explosion of the Web is . . . that it's open and anyone can publish content in the medium . . . I think that firms would like to stop that. For example, portals are an attempt to create centralized networks in a way that's borrowed from the traditional media. This idea keeps coming up in different formats."[3]

Hoffman believes that the idea of "pushing" content at passive consumers will not work ultimately and that advertising and marketing models based on traditional methods miss the point.

> "People are counting what they can count rather than asking, 'What should we count, and how can we figure out how to do that?' We should be counting interactivity ... not just somebody hitting a web page ... If I'm a manager, what I want to know is: 'Am I meeting my objectives and hitting my targets?' Even if you tell me how many people have seen my banner, I want to know how many of them will become my customers ... We know it's probably pretty close to none."[4]

Companies are becoming more sophisticated about how they market online. Affiliate programs, where a web publisher can provide relevant links to a retail Website such as Amazon, Dell, or CDNow, are more promising and less invasive forms of advertising. For the valuation perspective, however, it is notable that many online companies were evaluated on the basis of projections of future advertising revenue based on doubtful premises of how Internet users actually behave and without any common standards of measurement.

EVA ONLINE

EVA proponents contend that EVA applies just as much to e-companies as old-line firms. Pointing to the difficulties of realistically estimating the future cash flows of online business, EVA guru Joel Stern gives an example of how EVA figures can "do a better job of tracking the value" of an e-business.[5]

Between 1995 and 1998, RealNetworks Inc. showed annual losses as a percentage of sales of 88%, 29%, 40%, and 32%, despite gross profit growing from $1.75mn to $52.44mn. The losses derived from the high cost of selling, marketing, advertising and R&D. Stern believes (see Chapter 2) that these items are investments, rather than expenditure, and should be amortized over a realistic period, just as the cost of building a factory would be in a manufacturing company.

Amortizing these items over five years, Stern produced figures showing a net operating profit rising from $656,000 in 1995 to $29.13mn in 1998, with EVA averaging 40% for the period. He makes the point that traditional accounting measures reveal little about the performance of such companies because they are investing heavily to grow. EVA, he argues, helps us to assess whether the profits justify the amortized investment so far.

Defining the present value of expected future growth in EVA as future growth value (FGV), he states that most online companies have most of their current value in FGV, deriving from anticipated growth in existing products, anticipated growth from products in development and even from products not yet invented. FGV is so high principally because:

» the profit margins, as measured by EVA, are extremely high – variable costs can be as low as 15% of sales;
» e-businesses started small and grew extremely quickly.

CANNIBALIZING EXISTING INDUSTRIES

Some businesses seem tailor-made for the Internet, such as stock broking. Charles Schwab was the first large "bricks and mortar" broker to go almost completely online, and new competitors such as E*Trade and Ameritrade, sprang up to grab market share. At the time, this was hailed as farseeing because of the benefits to consumers in terms of lower fees and great access to information, combined with great increases in efficiency. Business boomed as new investors came into the market to trade online. By 2001, however, the excitement had begun to wear off. Schwab's trades in January 2001 were down 26% from January 2000, and it announced that it was cutting its workforce by more than 10%. Online competitors were also undertaking similar cost-cutting measures. Commentators suggested that these companies had over-invested to cope with expected growth in trading that failed to materialize.

Banking, another obvious candidate for going online, has been generally more cautious. Despite clear benefits in increased efficiency and improved customer service, this highly regulated industry has other concerns, such as the effects of mass layoffs and the needs of older customers who may not be familiar with the Internet. The expected transition may eventually take place, potentially adding enormous value. Banks, says Stern, ''have purchased the right, but not the obligation, to grow an internet banking service.''

The conclusion? It is too early to assess the value of many online activities – for many, the value is out there to be grasped, but new techniques must be developed to exploit the opportunities. It is not unlikely that there will be more e-booms in the future as online firms solve the problem of how to profit from cyberspace.

KEY POINTS

» Stock market booms are, by definition, periods when prices, usually in one particular sector, rise much higher than their underlying value. The valuations of some e-businesses may prove to be justified in the long term.
» During the e-boom, high values were justified on the basis of expectations about future earnings. Yahoo!, for example, was seen as likely to dominate the market for online advertising, which was growing rapidly. The advertising revenue model for online firms is now seen as questionable. Yahoo! and others are now seeking additional sources of income.
» Traditional mass advertising approaches have been based on aggressive shotgun methods. The interactive nature of the Internet, offering users more choice and the ability to self-publish, needs more sensitivity and relevance than, say, television advertising.

NOTES

1 Gough, L. (1999) *Trading the World's Markets*, John Wiley, Singapore
2 Gough, L. (2000), *Investing in Internet Stocks*, John Wiley, Singapore.

3 Gough, L. (2000), *Investing in Internet Stocks*, John Wiley, Singapore.
4 Gough, L. (2000), *Investing in Internet Stocks*, John Wiley, Singapore.
5 Stern, J. and Shiely, J. with Ross, I. (2001) *The EVA Challenge*, Wiley, New York.

The Global Dimension

Globalization presents huge valuation problems. A unified system is still a long way off. This chapter looks at:

» international accounting differences;
» cross-border valuation;
» BMW and Rover;
» emerging countries.

I know that we in America like to hold ourselves out as having great standards ... but I've been an investor for a little over thirty years and I'll tell you that at the end of the 1960s, for instance, American accounting was hopeless. Somehow, people were still able to invest in the stock market and make a living.

Jim Rogers, author of Investment Biker, one-time partner of Georges Soros[1]

As we saw in Chapter 1, there is resistance to the shareholder value philosophy in Asia and, more particularly, in Europe. Nevertheless, companies based in these regions often have foreign subsidiaries and undertake overseas joint ventures and mergers and acquisitions. These transactions require accurate valuations of businesses, despite major differences in accounting conventions, regulatory climate and business methods.

One item tends to remains the same in different countries – free cash. For this reason, discounted cash flow (DCF) is widely used for valuation purposes around the world in cross-border transactions. There is evidence that the ratio of DCF to book values do correlate quite closely to the ratio of stock prices to book value in many countries.

ACCOUNTING DIFFERENCES ACROSS THE WORLD

Many managers are astonished when they first learn how much accounting methods vary from country to country. The difference in standards is indeed staggering. Here are a few examples.

» Consolidated group accounts – some countries do not require consolidated accounts at all, while others insist that a parent company must consolidate its accounts with those of its subsidiaries. Definitions of a subsidiary vary greatly. In some countries, a subsidiary is a company that is 50% owned by the parent. In others, the figure is only 10%.
» The accounts in annual reports and those used for tax purposes do not always match because of differences in the accounting methods used, such as depreciation and deferred tax. This is the case in the USA.
» Many countries allow assets to be written-up to market value, which affects ratios such as return on capital.

» Goodwill, which in an acquisition is the difference between the price paid for a business and its assets, is sometimes written off immediately and sometimes written off over a long period. Its tax treatment diverges widely.

» In many cases, companies in the same country have a choice in how to treat items that significantly affect the balance sheet. This makes even domestic comparisons with competitors difficult.

A survey of 53 key countries' accounting measures in 2001 found that harmonization of local accounting practices with International Accounting Standards (IAS) was proceeding slowly despite efforts by the European Union and regulators elsewhere to force listed firms to conform to IAS. The USA's GAAP does not conform to IAS, and many foreign companies that have American Depository Receipts (ADRs) or are fully listed in the US markets must have two sets of books – one to meet US requirements and one for their home countries. Globalization is forcing the issue as capital flows more freely across borders, but the process is by no means complete, and may never be so. John M. Riley of Arthur Andersen says, "It does not make sense for companies reporting their information on the worldwide web to communicate in so many different, non-comparable financial reporting languages."[2]

It is not going to be easy. Professor Nelson Carvalho of the University of São Paulo, Brazil, who is an active member of several international accounting committees, has complained that rich nations don't always play by the rules, and allow ambiguities such as not forcing completely transparent disclosure of financial information for public offerings of stock. He points out that if the powerful nations don't play fair, "you can't expect emerging economies to do it."

Although making financial information publicly available to stock market investors is a common objective across the world, for some nations it is not the principal purpose of their accounting rules. In France and Germany, for instance, where the free market philosophy is not widely esteemed, accounts tend to be viewed chiefly as the means for calculating tax and dividends and as the basis for making business contracts. In France, the state relies heavily on the accounts of large companies to make macroeconomic decisions. In Germany, the maximum auditors' liability for audits of listed companies is only DM8mn which, some argue, indicates a weakness in enforcing the rules. There are also doubts about whether IAS will ever be truly enforceable internationally.

CROSS-BORDER VALUATION IN PRACTICE

The rule-makers may be doing their best, but in the meantime managers of large companies must deal effectively with the confusion that exists today.

To see how these problems are dealt with in practice, let's take the example of how a US parent might value a European subsidiary that borrows in several countries and generates revenues in, say sterling and Swiss francs.

The first step is to forecast the cash flow in the currencies in which they are received – sterling and Swiss francs. Numerous adjustments need to be made for tax and accounting differences. Then the cash flow is converted into the parent's domestic currency, using forward exchange rates as estimates. Next, the subsidiary's cost of capital is estimated and subtracted from the cash flow and finally the free cash flow is discounted and the present value converted into the home currency at the spot (current) exchange rate.

The struggles of the automobile industry illustrates how difficult cross-border valuations can be, even in an apparently "globalized" sector. In early 1998, Alex Trotman, then the CEO of Ford Motor Company, estimated auto manufacturing world over-capacity at 40%. Governments have contributed to this problem because of their aspirations to make their domestic manufacturers key players in this vital component of the world's economy and have resisted attempts to close local plants.

In Western Europe, the industry was virtually stagnating by the late 1990s, with analysts estimating regional over-capacity at 3.5–7 million vehicles, out of a total capacity of around 16 million. Increased competition from the Far Eastern manufacturers such as Japan, Malaysia and Korea were adding to the difficulties of over-supply.

European manufacturers tried hard to cut costs through increased efficiency, but were rapidly faced with the prospect of job cuts. Germany reduced its workforce by about a third from 1991 to 1994, while France and Sweden allowed factory closures following a failed merger attempt between Renault and Volvo. European governments frequently support their local manufacturers through subsidies, part ownership and erecting trade barriers. Protection of employment is seen as paramount in many quarters.

Analysts see the European industry as mature and relying almost exclusively on replacement purchases. Expansion into the newly open Eastern European countries has been hampered by competition from cheaper vehicles made in the Far East. Consolidation has been inevitable. Major European manufacturers numbered 47 in 1960 and had dropped to 17 in 1998, despite occasional spurts of growth, such as in the late 1980s.

BITING THE BULLET – BMW AND ROVER

In 1994 BMW purchased 80% of the troubled UK manufacturer Rover for £800mn, assuming debts of around £1bn. For BMW, Rover was attractive for several reasons:

» corporate average fuel economy (CAFÉ) rules threatened BMW's own high cost, large-engine products and it needed to reduce this risk by entering the small and medium car market segments;
» the purchase allowed the group to go down market while protecting the value of the BMW brand;
» Rover's Land Rover brand was seen as prestigious and valuable.

Sensitive to local pride and employment concerns, BMW attempted to manage Rover from a distance for the next four years, but despite investing some £2.5bn in the company, the hoped-for turnaround failed to materialize as losses grew. In 1997, operating losses were £98mn, rising to £650mn in 1998. The company cited falling sales, rising costs, new models, a strong pound, and the expense of restructuring.

In 1998 Rover began to cut jobs, and reduced the workforce by 19% in the following year. Losses increased in 1999 to £750mn and Rover's problems began to damage its parent – BMW's net income for the year was €663mn, but this was reduced to a loss of €2.49bn because of provisions to cover Rover's losses.

Differences between German and British accounting standards became highly contentious as a public quarrel erupted, further damaging Rover's sales. BMW claimed that Rover was losing £2mn a day, but critics argued fiercely that this did not reflect the true cash flow of the business. Sales of spare parts and customer financing deals were highly profitable, yet these revenues were diverted to BMW. BMW was accused of errors in foreign exchange management that caused a loss of £300mn as sterling rose against European currencies. In the UK, investment in plant and product development can be amortized over many years, yet BMW wrote off hefty sums in the years in which they occurred.

BMW hoped for substantial financial aid from the UK government, but it was not forthcoming, in part because of pressure from other manufacturers – the UK was much more in favor of free markets than it had been 20 years earlier, when a vicious cycle of labor problems and state subsidies had come to be known as "The British Disease."

Now the German media were calling Rover "The English Patient," after a popular movie, and the secretive Quandt family, owners of 46% of BMW, were said to be concerned that the problems could make the parent company a target for stock market predators.

Best practice

Corporate strategy in Europe can never be straightforward given the constraints of the stakeholder paradigm, and BMW's original strategy for the acquisition will probably never be fully known – did it calculate, for example, that a Labour Party in power in the UK would be forced to bail out Rover to prevent sizeable job cuts, as some claim? If so, it misjudged the mood of the times.

Whatever the truth of the matter, in 2000 BMW made a hugely value-creating decision: to sell the company. When it announced a deal to Alchemy Partners in March, BMW's stock price rose by 25%. That deal fell through, but after a prolonged negotiation process amidst wide publicity, including a public rally in Birmingham protesting job cuts that attracted 80,000 people, Rover was finally sold to a consortium named Phoenix. BMW's stock price has risen further, and its accounts showed record results in 2000.

DEVELOPING COUNTRIES

In developing countries, valuation becomes extraordinarily difficult. For instance, how do you value a listed company in a country with only six publicly quoted companies, all of which are in different industries? Decisions have to made without full information, and often with considerable political risk.

A Ukrainian balance sheet

Professor Alfred Steinherr, chief economist at the European Investment Bank, gives this example of the problems of valuing businesses in less developed countries:

"Recently I was considering the purchase of a bank in the Ukraine. I looked at the profit and loss statement and tried to evaluate what each [item] really meant. There was a big real estate item on the asset side [which] was the building in which the bank had its headquarters. The manager of the bank, who was also its major shareholder, was a Member of Parliament and had obtained the right, free of charge, to use the building, which in fact belonged to the state ... how do you evaluate such a thing? As long as this man is in political power, you have a big asset for free. As soon as he's out, or he sells up, it's worth nothing ... It was only through an indiscretion that I found out that the building didn't belong to the bank. It looked in the accounts as if it belonged to them. The refurbishing ... was paid by them, so it looked as if they were investing in their own building."[3]

Steinherr makes the point that at present in the former-USSR countries, it is futile to base decisions on company accounts: "Even the largest company in Russia gives you a balance sheet and a profit and loss statement that is totally meaningless."

Not all less developed countries (LDCs) are in such a perilous state. Mark Mobius, a fund manager at Franklin Templeton and a doyen of emerging market investment, has a list of some 40 LDCs that are "investable," in the sense that their stock markets are large enough to make it worthwhile for the fund to take the risk. The list includes countries such as Morocco, Egypt, and Peru. Mobius argues that the accounting system is imperfect in both the developed world and LDCs because the principle of independent auditing does not work:

"the people on whom we rely for ... independent information about companies are not really independent. The auditors are hired by the management. The auditors have consulting subsidiaries who sell their services to the management. That's a real flaw in the current system ... until that situation is resolved, we will always have to be suspicious about company accounts ... there is a great incentive to hide things."[4]

CORPORATE GOVERNANCE AND TRANSPARENCY

As globalization gathers pace, the need for good corporate governance and "transparency" has become a vital issue. To have a level playing field in capital markets, the interests of all investors, particularly minority investors, must be protected. In many regions, however, majority shareholders are able to conduct business in a way that would be regarded as an abuse in the USA. For example, in parts of Asia it is common for a family group to control a number of listed and unlisted companies. Business transactions between these related companies often raise serious conflicts of interest.

Since the 1997 Asian currency crisis, enormous pressure has been exerted on Asian countries to improve corporate governance and make the banking system more transparent. Thailand, South Korea, Indonesia and other nations were forced to borrow money from the International Monetary Fund (IMF), and were subjected to stringent conditions demanding structural reforms. Progress has been slow. A senior US diplomat who was active in promoting these reforms in South East Asia remarks that without the necessary changes, growth will be hard to sustain:

> "The banks are sitting there in many cases with non-performing loans that haven't been dealt with ... In some of the countries where we've seen non-performing loans go down, the question becomes, 'have the non-performing loans gone because of restructuring that'll have to be restructured again, or have they ... actually bitten the bullet?' You can't disguise inefficiency. You can't paint it over, it's still there ... Banks have lent into non-competitive entities and unless they are changed, then all you have done is defer a problem ... I'm concerned that a lot of the restructurings have put companies in that position."[5]

Along with the USA and Europe, Asia is one of the three major trading blocs in the world. For real globalization to occur, massive changes must take place. As the 1997 crisis illustrates, investment without an open and efficient system can lead to disaster.

KEY POINTS

» When accounting information in foreign countries is incomplete or impossible to interpret, discounted cash flow may be the only way to reach realistic valuations.

» Accounting practices vary considerably throughout the world, despite ongoing efforts to create harmonized standards. This makes it very difficult to value a company in an unfamiliar jurisdiction on the basis of its annual report.

» Even within developed countries, accounting differences cause problems; following its purchase of Rover, BMW's claim that Rover was making heavy losses was violently criticized in Britain. Opponents argued that under British accounting methods, Rover would have shown a profit.

» In some developing countries, accounting reports may be completely meaningless. However, respected investors have challenged the developed world's system, suggesting that independent audits are not always as independent as they should be.

» In rapidly developing economic regions such as Asia, corporate governance and transparency issues are crucial. Following heavy losses, investors are demanding wide-ranging reforms to the financial structure of the region.

» Globalization is a burgeoning trend, but from the point of view of valuing companies, there is a very long way to go before company information can be said to be truly "global."

NOTES

1 Rogers, J. (1994) *Investment Biker*, Random House, New York. Quote from Gough, L. (1999) *Trading the World's Markets*, John Wiley, Singapore.

2 Press release, Arthur Andersen, "New survey finds significant differences between national accounting rules and international accounting standards," Chicago, January 17, 2001.

3 Gough, L. (1999) *Trading the World's Markets*, John Wiley, Singapore.

4 Gough, L. (1999) *Trading the World's Markets*, John Wiley, Singapore.

5 In a conversation with the author.

The State of the Art

This chapter looks at some of the problems caused by poor valuation, and provides a detailed summary of what actions really do add measurable net value. The subject matter includes:

» stock analysts' failures;
» short-termism;
» the equity premium – why people make faulty decisions;
» creating a brand by creating customer value;
» predatory sales tactics;
» value enhancement in detail.

Decision makers do not consider all consequences of their alternatives. They focus on some and ignore others. Relevant information about consequences is not sought, and available information is often not used ... Instead of calculating the "best possible" action, they search for an action that is "good enough."

Professor James March, decision-making expert

THE PROBLEM WITH STOCK ANALYSTS

Legions of highly educated stock analysts using, for the main part, theoretically defensible techniques, do not do very well at estimating the future growth of the companies they study. In the USA, the average error for earnings per share predictions has been found to be just a few percentage points more accurate than a "naïve forecast" calculated using time series models – studies suggest that analyst errors are in the order of 16–30% over the medium to long term They tend to be slightly better at forecasting industry-wide EPS and large company EPS than other predictions. Most of the effort goes into forecasting the next quarter's earnings, although many analysts also estimate growth over the next five years, but with demonstrably less information.

A team of analysts chosen by Institutional Investor (the "All-America Analysts") have not been found to be significantly better forecasters than their colleagues, although their buy/sell recommendations have had a noticeable effect on stock prices, particularly for sell recommendations.

Analysts tend to make far more recommendations to buy than to sell – although some argue that "hold" is a euphemism for "sell." The explanation for emphasizing buys may be the close relationships that analysts have with the corporations they follow. This may also explain why analysts tend to think in herds and follow a consensus, both when making the recommendation and when earnings estimates are revised later.

Insider dealing rules prevent the unfair use of inside knowledge in stock investment, yet analysts are often presented as having access to special private knowledge about firms that others cannot access. The truth is probably the reverse of this; most of the information that analysts use is publicly available. Such private information as they do obtain is probably from the company itself and may be severely biased towards depicting the best possible outlook.

The conclusion? Analysts' EPS forecasts are not useless, but they are not much better than simply identifying the historical trend in a company's EPS growth rate.

SHORT-TERMISM

Shareholder value is, as we have seen, about using discounted estimates of future cashflows to arrive at an estimate of a company's worth (see Chapter 8 for the basics of how DCF is calculated) and then looking for ways of increasing that worth. It was never intended to be merely an increase in the company's stock price – stocks may fluctuate for all kinds of reasons that are nothing to do with intrinsic and sustainable long-term value. In recent years, however, short-term stock price gains have become a substitute for value creation in many quarters.

It all started with the leveraged buyout (LBO) craze of the 1980s. Using massive amounts of debt, LBO specialists were able to purchase large companies and radically restructure them to create short-term value, making fortunes in the process. To the extent that this process eliminated inefficiencies it was necessary, but waves of corporate downsizing, radical changes in core businesses through sales and acquisitions and, in some cases, stock buy-backs have potentially destroyed companies' earning potential in the long term.

Much of the pressure to focus on the short term comes from institutional investors. To a large extent, institutional investors are middlemen, employing the savings of millions of ordinary people to influence large corporations. In business themselves, they must sell their own expertise and capacity to make good returns to their own customers, the small investor. Professionally managed funds do not, overall, have an impressive track record in the medium to long term. As a group, they underperform the market – you would be better off "buying the index" in the form of a tracker fund that produces returns in line with a major stock market index. That's a near total failure in stock picking – professional investors have not, overall, demonstrated any superior ability at investing.

The blame does not rest entirely with the professionals. Stock markets, it is often said, run on fear and greed. Unsophisticated small investors hope to make quick fortunes in stocks, and have been increasingly willing to switch from one fund to another on the basis of recent performance. This puts enormous pressure on fund managers, especially those who are employees, rather than owner managers, of their funds, to switch investments rapidly in the search for short-term gains. Fund managers may feel confident that solid Company X will produce outstanding overall returns if they hold the stock for 10 years, but still be forced to switch to glamorous Company Y, today's stock market darling that may well crash drastically tomorrow. Not to do so could lose the fund huge numbers of customers.

With so much at stake, institutions have pressurized companies to focus on quarterly earnings reports. The slightest shortfall in earnings can trigger massive sell-offs and a consequent drop in stock price. Today, many are arguing that this practice does no-one any favors, since gains made in this way may cause larger losses in the future.

THE PROBLEM OF THE EQUITY PREMIUM

First raised in the 1980s, the equity premium question is "Why has the average real return on stocks equity been so much higher than interest rates?" This is a problem that traditional economic models cannot answer. These models assume that investors are rational and will, overall and in the long run, pay prices for stocks commensurate with the risk. Yet stock returns are much more volatile (liable to swings) than these models predict: rationally, stocks should mimic changes in consumption of goods and services, but consumption is actually much less volatile.

In 1996 Fed chief Alan Greenspan made his famous remark about the "irrational exuberance" of the stock market. For the next three years, however, stock prices continued to go up at a rapid rate with increasing volatility.

Prospect Theory (see Chapter 3), which looks at how people make decisions when there is uncertainty, sheds some interesting light on the problem. The theory's proponents, Daniel Kahneman and Amos Tversky have shown that people care more about the changes to their wealth than they do about its absolute value, and that they treat gains and losses differently.[1]

These ideas have been extended to develop a model that may explain the psychological dynamics behind stock market booms and busts. The essential proposition is that many investors are not rational but "loss averse," in contradiction to classical economic theory, and that they tend to overweight or underweight the probabilities when making decisions according to how rich or poor they are feeling. Loss averse investors are the reason for the increase in both returns and volatility in the stock market beyond what classical theory predicts.

More specifically, the argument is that when stocks are booming people who feel that they have already made substantial gains become willing to take bigger chances. They adopt what is in effect a "buy high, sell low" policy, because when stock prices reverse to a falling trend, they sell. While completely rational investors would keep a constant proportion of their wealth in stocks, loss averse investors tend to put more of their wealth into the market.

When things start to go bad, loss averse investors alter their behavior, becoming risk-avoiding. They now decrease volatility by acting as contrarians, buying stocks at low prices and thereby helping to stabilize them, in the expectation that returns will eventually revert to the long-term average. This is the exact opposite of their behavior at the top of the market, when their actions imply that they expect future returns to diverge from the long-term average.

When things get very bad indeed, loss averse investors get out of the stock market altogether, making prices go very low. The only buyers are rational investors who expect that returns will eventually revert to the long-term average, and therefore regard depressed stocks as bargains.

CREATING VALUE FOR THE CUSTOMER

Turning shareholder value into a short-termist obsession with improving earnings figures is essentially inward-looking. It ignores the essence of any business, developing sales and customer loyalty. While there is nothing new about this, Delivering Profitable Value (DPV), a proprietary strategy approach developed by the consultant Michael J. Lanning, sheds some interesting light on ways of creating value that are outside the province of the Finance Department.[2]

DPV emphasizes focusing on the customer experience as a way of creating a superior "value proposition." Lanning says that this is often a trade-off between benefits and disadvantages. For instance, the VHS videotape format was inferior in picture quality to its rival Betacam, but delivered a superior value proposition: you could rent a much wider variety of movies on VHS than on Betacam. Too often, he argues, companies think about selling the benefits they perceive internally ("our picture quality is better") than what people really want (lots of movies).

By detailed analysis of customer experiences, for example, by videotaping their behavior, DPV seeks to find ways of offering superior value. The proposition is not enough on its own, but must be integrated with a "value delivery system" requiring the coordination of the process by which the product reaches the end customer. Lanning uses the example of Perdue Farms, a small chicken producer, to illustrate this.

In the 1960s, Perdue Farms was a commodity business supplying wholesalers and supermarket chains with frozen chickens. At the time, the focus was on the immediate customer, (the wholesaler/retailer), rather than on the ultimate consumer who actually ate the chicken. Perdue made efforts to analyze the consumer experience in a search for ways of adding value to its product and discovered that people had a preference for chickens with a golden yellow skin, which they associated with tender meat, and would be willing to pay a premium for such a product. Going further, Perdue decided to actually supply tender chickens – not merely golden yellow chickens that looked as if they might be tender – by distributing them fresh, not frozen.

This was regarded as a retrograde step by the industry at the time. Distributing fresh chickens involved considerable extra cost and was perceived as technologically backward. Perdue began by concentrating on upmarket butchers, having already established that some consumers would go out of their way to purchase superior chickens from these stores.

Having built a reputation for superior quality through the high-class butchers, Perdue was then able to approach supermarkets with proof of the demand for the product. The company took another innovative step by advertising its products on television, using Frank Perdue, the CEO, as the spokesman to explain to consumers how the company fed their chickens on better food, had exacting quality standards and delivered the chickens fresh, not frozen, to the stores and ending with the amusing slogan, "It takes a tough man to make a tender chicken." The advertising was effective and supermarkets overcame their initial reluctance to stock more expensive chickens. A successful brand was born.

SOME DUBIOUS TACTICS

It is possible to increase shareholder value by instituting sharp practice in dealing with customers, but whether this is really value creating in the long term is, to say the least, doubtful.

Examples abound in IT. For example, Microsoft offered two versions of its Windows NT software, one priced three to four times higher than the other, which analysts claim are almost identical although the company disputes this. On the hardware side, IBM produced a cheap laser printer that printed five pages a minute in contrast to the higher cost printers that printed 10 pages a minute. The only difference between the machines was that the cheap version contained a chip to slow down the printing process! This fact was soon discovered and publicized by techie consumers.

With the commoditization of air travel, confusion pricing has become notorious in the airline industry. Airlines operate complex price structures that are clearly designed to deceive all but the most determined ticket buyer into paying more than necessary. Consumer TV shows frequently publicize this, telling stories of irate consumers who have discovered that they have paid double what the passenger in the seat next to them has paid for the same journey. Online ticket sellers have ticket cartel-busting as a stated objective although it is noticeable that some online agents have adopted similar confusion tactics.

Differential pricing, the practice of varying prices in different retail outlets, is becoming increasingly common. The rationale is that the individual consumer may not notice, and if they do, they are too small on their own to make a difference. While this may be true, it is not evident that this is a good method of creating goodwill and loyalty.

Customer loyalty has been on the wane in recent years according to numerous surveys. A study of 500 brands in 1996 by NPD Group found that only 12% of customers were "highly loyal to any brand." Other research indicates significant drops in brand loyalty and the perception of brand value in many areas, ranging from food to travel products. A writer on customer loyalty, Frederick Reichheld, claims that "on average, US corporations lose half their customers in five years, half their employees in four and a half, their investor in less than one."[3]

The Internet may have the effect of commoditizing many products because it makes it easier for customers to compare prices. Some pundits argue that consumers' increasing focus on low prices is a response to deceptive selling practices such as those outlined above. Certainly part of the attraction of the Internet to consumers is the ability to receive and share information about products and services independently of organizations – both commercial and in the public sector – that have hitherto been concealed.

VALUE ENHANCEMENT: THE FINANCIAL VIEWPOINT

In financial terms, the factors that create value are straightforward.

1 Generating higher cash flows from existing assets will increase value.
2 Reinvesting earnings can lead to value-adding growth.
3 Reducing the cost of capital will increase value. Conversely, the more your borrowing costs you, the less your firm will be worth.

Each element affects the others. For example, if you are trying to increase cash flows from your existing business, you must ensure that this does not damage the potential for growth too much, or raise your risk profile excessively to lenders. Almost invariably there have to be trade-offs – a little more risk, say, for a lot more cashflow.

For investors, one extra element is needed. It is not enough just to calculate how much value a company has created; you must also compare it with the expectations of the stock market. Investors usually only obtain above average returns when the company produces results that are better then market expectations.

Increasing value is easier said than done, especially in competitive markets. When it is achieved, it is usually because of hard-to-measure factors such as excellent management, powerful marketing, shrewd decisions or a good brand. Clearly, unless the management makes adding value its top priority, it is unlikely to occur. There are hidden dangers here, because if managers concentrate on enhancing performance based on a single measure, they may unwittingly destroy real value.

Existing businesses

Before undertaking any new projects, you should look at what can be done with the existing businesses. Can they be managed better? Are they earning as much as, or more than, their cost of capital?

With businesses that earn less than their true cost of capital, the most obvious answer is to either sell them as going concerns or to liquidate them. Usually, however, liquidating a business will not return the capital you have invested. To decide which course to take, or whether it is better to keep the business going, work out which of the following is higher:

1 the price you can obtain by selling the business;
2 the price you can obtain by liquidating the business;
3 the net present value (NPV; see Chapter 8) of future cash flows.

If the NPV is higher than the price for liquidation or sale, then you will destroy less value by keeping the business going, even if it is not earning its cost of capital.

» *Improving efficiency.* Are you able to make your operations more efficient? One way to judge this is by comparing your operating margins with those of similar competitors. If the margin is much lower, it is *prima facie* evidence that it can be improved, perhaps by cutting costs or reducing staff. These actions can only work if earnings are improved or growth potential is unaffected. Suspending all advertising, training and R&D, for instance, is likely to be damaging rather than value enhancing.

» *Reduce inventory and trade credit.* Retailers are especially vulnerable to cash drains from holding too much inventory, but many businesses can increase efficiency in this area by such techniques as just-in-time delivery. Giving customers time to pay may be necessary to make sales, but there is often room for improvement, for example by offering a discount for early payment, or tightening credit terms for new customers. These measures have to be considered carefully;

if they result in too many lost sales, they may be value-destroying. The use of IT to plan better has had a positive effect in recent years, with large companies reducing non-cash working capital (principally inventory and credit) by about 3% during the 1990s. That 3% reduction directly becomes a 3% increase in cash flow.

» *Cutting tax.* As we will see in Chapter 7, Rupert Murdoch's News Corp has enjoyed, entirely legally, very low taxes for many years through exploiting international tax loopholes; it pays much less taxes than its major media competitors in the USA, which is its major source of revenue. Any company with businesses in more than one country has the potential to reduce tax by moving revenue through subsidiaries in low tax or no tax jurisdictions. Other possibilities include buying an unprofitable business to use up tax loss allowances or using financial risk management techniques to "smooth" income so that it falls into a lower tax band in several years.

» *Cutting net capital spending.* Capital spending is done to maintain existing assets and to create future growth. Reducing maintenance spending will often shorten the life of an asset, but not always. It is a trade-off, but if you can reduce the capital expenditure below depreciation charges, cash flow will increase.

Growth

Growth comes from investing more in a business or from getting a better return. It does not necessarily create value, since a risky new venture may increase the cost of capital and higher re-investment of cash may reduce cash flows. Here are the possible strategies.

» *Buying businesses.* Acquisitions only add value if they produce a higher return on the cost of capital, a fact of life that was forgotten in innumerable twentieth-century mergers. Many studies have found that acquisitions of listed companies rarely result in a return that is better than the cost of capital; in very many cases acquisitions have been value-destroying. Buying privately owned companies is more likely to add value because the purchase premium will generally be lower, there will rarely be a bidding war and there may be genuine synergies.

Investment bankers make a lot of money out of advising on public company mergers and acquisitions, and executives may benefit from a subsequent increase in their power and compensation. This is not the same as creating value for the firm – acquisitions are really just another investment, and can be judged by the same criteria. To create value, the net present value of the combined company must be higher than the cost of acquisition.

» *Change prices.* There are two basic pricing strategies. The first, raising your prices, will increase profit margins but often reduces sales. The second is to lower prices in the hope of increasing sales. In many cases, they are not short-term fixes; it may take years for the full effects to manifest.

It is difficult to value the effects of these strategies in advance because you do not know exactly how the competition will respond. If you cut your prices you may start a price war with the competition that results in lower margins and lower sales volume – a value-destroying outcome. Price cutting may be more effective if your company has, or can create, a sustainable cost advantage over your competitors.

Higher prices may be accepted by your market if you are building a brand, or if there is high demand. To add value, the effect of the price increase must be greater than the loss of sales.

» *Reinvest more.* The key here is to ensure that reinvesting from earnings actually produces growth. The NPV of the extra cash flows must be higher than the NPV of the increase in reinvestment.

» *Raise the return on capital.* If your company has businesses where the return on capital is less than the cost of capital, you can add value if you can improve the returns by investing more, but liquidating all or part of the business and repaying the capital could well be more value enhancing.

If you are able to invest in new projects that increase returns without raising the cost of capital, you will add value. Even if the cost of capital for the new businesses is higher, you will still add value if the returns exceed the cost of capital.

The cost of capital

The capital of a firm consists of borrowings and money raised by the sale of stock. The net present value of future cash flows is calculated by estimating their value today (what is $1,000 coming in two years' time worth in today's money?), and discounting them at the same rate as the cost of capital (see Chapter 8). Even if there are no changes to the future cash flows of the business, you could still create value by reducing the cost of capital, possibly by changing the proportion of lending and equity or changing the type of debt.

» *Changing the type of debt*. Ideally, the payments that a company must make for its debt should mimic cash flows in as closely as possible. It can support higher debt repayments at times when there is more cash coming in, so there may be scope to add value by more efficient management of short-term borrowing. The classic mistake is to use short-term debt to finance long-term investment; because this debt must be repaid before the returns from the investment arrive, it can create a cash crisis. Cash flow problems can also occur if the debt and the returns are in different currencies and the exchange rates turn against you. Short-term debt tends to have a variable rate of interest, so an increase in inflation will raise its cost, often before it is possible to raise prices in compensation. Debt "mismatches" of these types can be mitigated by using financial derivatives such as currency swaps (but see Chapter 3, Derivatives).

Optimising debt payments to match cash inflows adds value.

» *Cut fixed costs*. High fixed costs ("overheads") mean a higher cost of capital and fluctuating earnings. Outsourcing has the effect of turning fixed costs into variable costs – you only buy it when you need it – but the cost of the service may be higher, so you need to assess whether outsourcing is worthwhile. In countries with heavy employment protection, outsourcing many services that would otherwise be done by expensive employees in-house who are difficult to remove may add an enormous amount of value. Some countries frown on this practice.

Salaries are often the highest fixed cost in a company. In jurisdictions that allow it, tying salaries to earnings performance as far as possible helps to reduce fixed costs.

» *Reducing customer risk*. Some businesses rely heavily on a small number of customers or on a single small market. This is risky, since sales may fall suddenly because of a customer decision – for instance, suppliers to large retail chains often experience this. Diversifying into new markets and customer bases reduces this risk, and will, over time, create value.

» *Altering the proportion of debt to equity*. It may not be obvious at first glance, but finance theory tells us that debt is cheaper than equity because of tax advantages and a lower cost of capital. On the other hand, too much debt increases the risk of insolvency and makes stockholders' earnings fluctuate more widely. More debt may also affect cash flow negatively. The key is to optimize the debt/equity mix to create value.

High growth, high returns

Despite wishful thinking, most businesses eventually stabilize and grow at the same rate as the economy. In the short term, businesses are unlikely to sustain high returns for long where there is competition, since these high returns will attract more competitors and drive returns down.

A major question for managers is how to extend the time that a business can earn high returns. One way is to have barriers to entry, or, put another way, major competitive advantages. Very well established brands, for instance, act as barriers to entry (most people would not choose a generic cola over a name brand). In the pharmaceutical industry, the very high cost of drug development and the arduous FDA drug approval process (see Chapter 7, Genentech) act as barriers to entry. Patents, licenses, trademarks, and copyrights all serve as barriers to entry, but generally have a limited life. Monopolistic situations created by state regulation or contracts are also barriers to entry, but may not enhance value because the state may control prices.

Adding to, extending, and creating barriers to entry are among the most powerful ways of adding value to a business. They also tend to be expensive long-term undertakings. Much management science is rightly devoted to this subject. The potential rewards are out there – the challenge is to attain them.

KEY POINTS

» Professional investment analysts and fund managers are not, as a group, very good at valuing investments, probably because of biases inherent in their business.

» People tend to misjudge probabilities when taking decisions. Prospect Theory suggests that these errors are to some extent predictable.

» Do predatory pricing tactics create value in the long term?

» There are many ways to enhance value, almost always involving trade-offs between different financial factors. Careful analysis can reveal which actions are likely to be right for your company.

NOTES

1 For more information on Prospect Theory, see: Kahneman, D., Slovic, P. and Tversky, A. (eds.) (1982) *Judgement under Uncertainty: Heuristics and Biases*, Cambridge University Press, Cambridge; Kahneman, D. and Tversky, A. (1973) "On the psychology of prediction," *Psychological Review*, 80: 237–51; and Kahneman, D. and Tversky, A. (1979) "Prospect theory: An analysis of decision under risk," *Econometrica*, 263–91.

2 Lanning, M.J. (1998) *Delivering Profitable Value*, Perseus, New York.

3 Reichheld, F.F. (1996) *The Loyalty Effect*, Harvard Business School Press, Boston MA.

In Practice: Valuation Success Stories

The great long-term value creators are illustrated here:

» News Corporation;
» Genentech;
» Nokia.

"I have never seen anybody more astute at manipulating politicians to his advantage than Rupert."
Gus Fischer, a senior employee of Rupert Murdoch's News Corp.

NEWS CORPORATION

In the 1950s Rupert Murdoch inherited control of News Ltd, the owner of two small Australian newspapers, from his father. Over the subsequent half-century he has built News Corporation (News Corp.) into the third largest media conglomerate in the world, with annual sales of more than US $11bn. He has achieved this extraordinary growth largely through aggressive acquisition financed by debt, while retaining 30% of the stock in family ownership.

Empire-building through debt is not necessarily value-creating, but Murdoch's case may be an exception to the rule. Widely unpopular within the media industries, he nevertheless has displayed a profound grasp of the business, a talent for successful innovation and a shrewd and credible vision of how the media will develop in the future.

The deals were small at first. In 1956, News Ltd purchased a third Australian newspaper, and in the following year it launched *TV Week*, which was the inspiration for the highly successful *TV Guide* in the USA. *TV Week* became the most profitable of all of the company's Australian publications. In 1958, News Ltd took its first move out of newspapers by acquiring control of a small TV station in Adelaide. Murdoch established a pattern that he would follow for much of his life; replacing a large proportion of senior managers and staff, he would ease his personal supervision after a period of close involvement and generally the acquired company's results would improve.

During the 1960s, Murdoch built up a conglomerate of Australian newspapers, aiming for large market share. By 1968 News Corp. was large enough to purchase the UK's downmarket Sunday paper, the *News of the World*, followed by its main daily rival, the *Sun*, in 1969, giving him effective control of the blue collar newspaper market in the UK. He built the circulation of the *News of the World* from 1 million to 3 million between 1969 and 1973. Twenty years later, it had grown to be the largest selling English-language newspaper in the world.

In the 1970s, News Corp. embarked on acquisitions in its third target territory: the USA. It scored a major success by turning around the *New York Post* with its sensationalized covering of the "Son of Sam" murders and made money by acquiring the daily San Antonio papers in Texas, which were a monopoly in their local market. Other purchases of newspapers in major cities, such as Chicago and Boston, were loss-making but were financially supported by some successful magazines, particularly in New York.

Murdoch did not become widely noticed until the early 1980s when he started purchasing well-known media companies, including the upmarket *The Times* and *Sunday Times* newspapers in the UK (1981) and Twentieth Century Fox in the USA (1985). The Fox purchase cost $575mn, a huge increase on his previous acquisitions. He also tried to gain control of Warner Communications, for a short time becoming its largest stockholder, and attempted an abortive bid for CBS television. Following these unsuccessful bids, he managed to purchase Metromedia, the leading group of non-network US TV stations, becoming a US citizen in order to gain regulatory approval.

In 1986 Murdoch took advantage of political developments in the UK to move his newspapers to a new plant, introducing new technology that the traditionally difficult print unions had strongly resisted. After a period of bloody and dramatic riots, Murdoch was successful, adding £60mn in annual profits to his group.

In 1987, Murdoch reacted to Australian legislation introduced to prevent ownership of both television and newspapers by selling his TV interests profitably and purchasing two further newspaper groups, giving him over 50% of the Australian newspaper market. He also moved into publishing, buying Harper & Row in the USA and Collins in the UK, costing a total of $1bn, to become a major international player. In 1988 he purchased Triangle in the USA, a magazine group that included *TV Guide*, *Seventeen* and *Daily Racing Form*, all titles that had a dominant position in their respective markets. The purchase price was $2.85bn.

Escaping bankruptcy

By 1988, Murdoch's short-term debts to banks were a massive $7bn. Like so many ambitious entrepreneurs before him, his huge borrowings made his company vulnerable to an economic downturn. This duly came in the following year, when the lenders themselves came under pressure and proved reluctant to roll over loans. Says Murdoch, "At no time were we not making good profits ... that more than covered our interest payments." This was not enough, however, when competing media were vigorously attacking News Corp. and banks were trying to get out of risky loans.

Although consistently profitable, News Corp. looked risky – in 1988/9, its short-term loans had increased by 600%. Citibank, News Corp.'s lead lender, tried to restructure the loans, but the other 144 banks involved were resistant. A bank in Pittsburgh initially refused to roll over a $5.1mn loan and nearly pushed the firm into insolvency. With $2bn due in January 1991 that had already been rolled over once, News Corp. was in serious trouble – two months before the deadline, there was still no restructuring deal in sight. The deal was eventually signed, largely because of Citibank's backing and Murdoch's track record. "If I'd ever stiffed a bank or done anything like that, I wouldn't have gotten through it," he says. "Reputations come with a lifetime of work."[1]

For the first time, News Corp. showed a loss – $393mn for the 1991 financial year. Murdoch vigorously reduced his debt, selling off the least important assets, refinancing when interest rates began to drop, and, most importantly, raising $700mn by a public offering that reduced his ownership from 43% to 35%. By 1992, News Corp. was back in profit and has continued to purchase media properties aggressively since then.

Today, News Corporation operates in many media on six continents with a diversified income spread between TV (including satellite), movies, book publishing, magazines and newspapers. Although most of its income is derived from the US, it continues to expand in continental Europe, Asia and Latin America, whose media industries are less developed and likely to enjoy faster growth.

KEY INSIGHTS

» Entrepreneurs like Rupert Murdoch challenge some valuation conventions because they are, in effect, owner-managers, unlike the executives in most large companies, and so are naturally interested in shareholder value. Murdoch uses debt to grow because it enables him to retain control; public offerings might be "cheaper" money, but it would force fundamental changes to his way of doing business. Aggressive growth is much harder to achieve when a committee is in charge – and Murdoch's board, say insiders, ratify his decisions rather than control them.

» Murdoch has been compared with buccaneering entrepreneurs who eventually came to grief, such as Robert Maxwell, but there is a fundamental difference in his approach: Murdoch is focused on profit-making, micro-management and value creation above all else. Speaking to New York analysts in 1988, he described his methods:

"Every day I receive print outs from each country on each operation item by item. Every newspaper, every magazine, every issue, a profit and loss covering the operation up to, and including, the previous Sunday. On Fridays those sheets are followed by thick books with itemised details of profit and loss figures on every single operation whether it be from Perth in Western Australia or in London or San Antonio. These figures are what keep us up to date. We compare them with previous years and compare it with our budget and take whatever management action is called for. We do it very simply, [with] very low overheads [and a] very small head office here in New York. What we do it with is management information and for that we spare nothing. We operate the company with weekly information. We can do this because of modern communications which we use not just for our customers but for our internal communications."

» A rapid series of M&A often fails because the hoped-for "synergies" fail to materialize. The media industries, however, are uniquely suited to synergistic acquisitions, first because of the huge global demand for product and access and second because traditional media, such as newspapers, were ripe for reform. While the US remains the most important market for the media, demand in the rest of the world keeps on growing and content generated in the US can be sold again and again in other territories and in new forms. Murdoch has generally been able to significantly improve the sales and profitability of his purchases.

» The media are among the most political of all industries because of their power over public opinion. Murdoch is widely regarded by both friends and enemies as being extremely successful in forming alliances with politicians of many political hues to further his business objectives.

» As a truly globalized group, News Corp. has legally exploited the lack of international tax harmony to reduce its tax burden. During the 1990s, News Corp.'s tax rate overall averaged 5.7%, a fifth of the tax paid by its major US competitors. This is achieved by channelling profits through dozens of subsidiaries in low-tax or no-tax jurisdictions such as the Cayman Islands and the Dutch Antilles. The company has nearly 800 business units incorporated in 52 countries, including Bermuda, Mauritius and Cuba.

» Murdoch has also taken full advantage of international differences in accounting to paint the best picture. The company remains Australian, which allows it to revalue its assets, such as TV shows, each year. US GAAP would force these to be shown at cost and to be depreciated each year. US accounting rules would reduce News Corp.'s shareholder equity by as much as 50%, some argue, and require the company to report net losses in some years.

» Investors invariably begin to worry about the succession as highly effective businesspeople age. Now 70, Murdoch has groomed some of his children to lead the business and by all accounts they are highly effective. Whether they will continue to expand the company as aggressively in the future cannot be known. When Murdoch eventually passes away, News Corp.'s nature may change fundamentally.

» A spokesman for Stern Stewart, the inventors of EVA, has criticized News Corp. recently, saying that adding MVA through increasing the stock price is not the same as creating EVA. Recent acquisitions have not yet increased earnings proportionately, and News Corp.'s EVA seems to be falling. The company is under pressure to make new ventures like Sky Global, a satellite broadcaster, succeed.

TIMELINE FOR RUPERT MURDOCH AND NEWS CORPORATION

» **1954**: Aged 23, Murdoch inherits two small Australian newspapers. Over the next few years, Murdoch expands into magazines, radio and television.

» **1969**: Murdoch buys the *News of the World* and the *Sun* in London, England, increasing their appeal through titillation and transforming them into highly profitable cash cows.

» **1981**: Murdoch buys *The Times* and the *Sunday Times*, Britain's most respected newspapers.

» **1985**: News Corp. buys Twentieth Century Fox Film Corp. and seven television stations from Metromedia Inc., turning them into Fox Television. Murdoch becomes an American citizen.

» **1986**: Murdoch moves his UK newspapers to modern facilities in Wapping and print unions strike violently. Eventually successful, Murdoch has transformed the highly inefficient UK newspaper industry. News Corp. is listed on the New York Stock Exchange.

» **1990**: News Corp.'s huge debts cause financial trouble. Citibank, the lead lender, tries to save the company from bankruptcy.

» **1991**: Murdoch sells most of his US magazines to raise money, retaining *TV Guide* and *Mirabella*. A refinancing deal covers $7.6bn in short and medium-term debt. News Corp. loses $393mn.

» **1992**: News Corp. completes a $700mn stock sale that eases the company's financial pressures, but reduces Murdoch's stake in the company from 43% to 35%. News Corp. makes a profit of $502mn in 1992.

» **1993**: Murdoch pays $525mn for 63.6% of Hong Kong-based Star TV, a satellite system that covers most of Asia. In the US, he pays $1.6bn for the rights to broadcast pro football on Fox TV.

» **2001**: Investors are hopeful that Murdoch will at last succeed in making satellite TV work. He seems close to finalizing a deal with Hughes Electronics to merge its DirecTV with News Corp.'s Sky Global empire to create a $70bn public company. If completed, the deal would give Murdoch's broadcast satellite empire a dominant market position worldwide.

GENENTECH

Medical biotechnology has had a checkered history since its commercial beginnings some 25 years ago, with many drug development companies failing after investing millions in compounds that did not pass the stringent approval process of the Food and Drug Administration (FDA) in the US. It is a high-risk business, with a huge profit potential for a winning drug. Genentech was the first biotech firm to be formed, and is one of the very few to have succeeded in creating compounds with $1bn in sales, the Holy Grail of the industry.

It all started when, in 1972, researchers found enzymes that could act as "molecular scissors" to cut out a gene from a strand of DNA and attach it to a different strand. In the following year scientists Herb Boyer and Stanley Cohen successfully transferred genes from a toad into bacteria and showed that the genes were inherited by later generations of the bacteria, still fully functioning. Genetic engineering was born.

In 1975 a young venture capitalist, Bob Swanson persuaded Herb Boyer to meet for ten minutes in a bar, but the two men became so enthused by the commercial potential of gene splicing that they agreed to start a company, Genentech, to exploit it.

Later entrants to biotech have complained that Genentech and other pioneer companies had it easy – they could pick the "low-hanging fruit" of the easiest, most obvious candidates for the new technology. This ignores the major regulatory hurdles that existed at the time and the extreme opposition from many scientists in the field, who had doubts about the wisdom of mass-producing genetically engineered products.

Swanson attracted scientists to work at Genentech by offering them a uniquely flexible employment package. Says Jean Deleage, a founder investor.

"They offered them the chance of making more money, access to the equipment they wanted, the freedom to work completely flexible hours, the chance to publish papers in their own names. They were willing to accept any arrangement for scientists to move back and forth between the company and universities ... [they] offered quite generous stock option plans to the scientists. The money wasn't all kept for the management and the business guys."[2]

Genentech's first success was in producing genetically engineered insulin. Insulin, used to treat millions of diabetics around the world, was at the time in dangerously short supply. For 60 years insulin had been obtained from animals, mainly cattle and pigs, which can cause adverse reactions in humans. In 1978, Genentech managed to synthesize human insulin by inserting the gene for human insulin into bacterial DNA. This meant that insulin could now be produced cheaply in vast quantities.

Humulin, as the commercial product was called, revolutionized diabetes treatment when it became widely available in the early 1980s. In 2000, Humulin achieved $1.11bn in sales. Almost all diabetics now use genetically engineered human insulin instead of animal insulin.

The "deal with the devil"

Today, Genentech does not receive any royalties from the sale of Humulin. In the late 1970s, the drug company Eli Lilly was a leading supplier of insulin, deriving it from pigs, but internal projections showed that growing demand would outstrip the material Lilly could produce by around 1992. Lilly invited a number of researchers to try to develop genetically engineered human insulin, promising a contract to the winner.

Genentech was the only commercial enterprise to compete (the others were universities), but it won the race and obtained the first ever contract between a biotech company and a giant pharmaceutical company.

In hindsight, it might look as if Genentech gave too much away. As with other early biotech/pharma alliances, the pharma, with its deep pockets and established marketing channels, had the upper hand.

Litigation followed, with Genentech finally receiving a settlement of $145mn in 1995.

The value of the deal was much more than an issue of royalties, however. It established the potential of what is now a vast industry with thousands of companies, and enabled Genentech to raise finance by proving that deals were possible – at the time, Wall Street was very doubtful that small-time entrepreneurs could get anywhere in a world dominated by slow-moving, highly bureaucratic drug companies and universities. Biotechs are in a much better negotiating position today but only, many say, because of Bob Swanson's original entrepreneurial vision.

Human growth hormone

In 1979, Genentech, working with University of California researchers, synthesized human growth hormone, which is needed for muscle formation and the breakdown of fats, which obtained FDA approval in 1985. This was Protropin, the first genetically engineered drug to be invented, made and sold by a biotech company – hitherto, the conventional wisdom was that only the major pharmas were capable of doing this. Protropin was used for children with growth hormone deficiency who had previously been treated at vast expense by hormone extracted from human cadavers. A further benefit was that the necessary injections were reduced from daily to just once or twice a month.

Genentech went public in 1980, raising $35mn and setting a record when shares jumped from $35 to $88 in less than an hour. By 2001, adjusting for several stock splits but not including cash payouts, Genentech's shares were worth more than 50 times their lowest price in 1980.

Enter Roche

By 1990, despite these and other successes, Genentech was in financial trouble. The company had a potential blockbuster drug called TPA, a treatment for heart attack patients, but it was not selling well, and Genentech was running out of cash for essential R&D. Bob Swanson's dream had always been to create a truly independent biotech company; this depended on having an ever-increasing pipeline of new products. The only way out was to find a partner.

The Swiss drug giant Roche was finding that its own research programs were unproductive and agreed to purchase 60% of the company for $2.1bn, with an option to buy the rest of the stock at a later date. Conscious that Genentech's success in discovery depended on the freedom it gave its scientists, Roche agreed to a hands-off approach, taking only two seats on the board and signing a strict governance deal. Some talented researchers did leave in disgust to start their own firms, but the majority stayed, and new discoveries continued to flow.

In 1995, Roche's option to buy the rest of the company was extended, but the deal changed to reduce Genentech's take of foreign sales of various drugs to royalties only. In a complex maneuver in 1999/2000, Roche exercised its option to buy the whole company, but then reissued shares on the New York stock exchange. Roche now owns around 58% of the company. Bob Swanson, the founder, tragically died from brain cancer in 1999.

In 2001, Genentech celebrated its 25th anniversary. With over 4,000 employees and hundreds of millions of dollars in annual sales, it increasingly resembles the large pharmas that it once sought to challenge. Competition and endless lawsuits make the struggle to bring new drugs to market endlessly difficult, but it has some winners, such as Rituxan, a treatment for non-Hodgkin's lymphoma; Activase a blood-clot treatment for heart attack and stroke victims; Protropin and Nutropin for growth hormone-related conditions); and Herceptin, a breast cancer drug. At least a dozen drugs are in the pipeline. Like many of its rivals, some of which, such as Amgen, have grown even larger than Genentech, much of its focus is on finding treatments for cancer, the greatest killer in the developed world.

KEY INSIGHTS

» The drug industry's most notable characteristic is that the FDA approval process serves as a very high barrier to entry, but also provides a form of monopoly for a successful drug, albeit limited by patent life and the risk of better treatments emerging. By the late twentieth century, new technology was perhaps the only way that a start-up company could become a major player in the industry, since it was only through new technology that it could hope to create effective compounds quickly enough to satisfy its investors by obtaining FDA approval. Bob Swanson's genius was in overcoming the initial resistance to genetic engineering to found what became a $30bn company. Says his ex-partner, Jean Deleage, now a leading biotech venture capitalist:

"Bob persuaded various important scientists to help him and then, with his naïve appearance and arguments, he was able to convince people that the benefits of biotechnology outweighed the risks by far. To my mind, that's the most important aspect of the creation of Genentech. Bob Swanson and the people around him were very ambitious but they knew how to be very humble towards the scientists. He was a good communicator to the outside world and he knew how to raise money."[3]

» At a time when medical research was dominated by the bureaucracy of large organizations, Swanson took the imaginative leap of being extremely generous and open to the researchers he hired, both in working practices and in profit participation. Without this generosity, progress would have been far slower and scientists would have been far more reluctant to risk their careers in an unproven industry. Like the "open source" philosophy among software developers, which enabled Netscape and Linux to grow rapidly because they were given away for free, this approach struck many as crazy at the time. It was probably the key decision in successfully creating one of the world's largest companies.

TIMELINE FOR GENENTECH

» **1976**: Robert Swanson and Dr Herbert Boyer found Genentech
» **1978**: Genentech clones human insulin
» **1979**: Genentech clones human growth hormone
» **1980**: The company raises $35mn in an IPO.

> » **1982**: Human insulin goes on sale, licensed by Genentech to Eli Lilly.
> » **1990**: Genentech and Roche merge, with Roche purchasing 60% of the company for $2.1bn. The company obtains FDA approval for a Hepatitis B vaccine and Activase, a treatment for blood clots in the lungs.
> » **1995**: Eli Lilly settles out of court with Genentech over human growth hormone. Roche extends its option to buy Genentech outright.
> » **1999/2000**: Roche buys up all outstanding Genentech shares, then conducts a new IPO, eventually selling off 42% of the company.

NOKIA

Nokia has created enormous value and become one of the world's top brands, despite being from Finland, a country of a little over 5 million people that has always been caught between much more powerful neighbors.

It is a remarkable story. Nokia started out in the late nineteenth century as a paper mill that expanded rapidly through international exports at a time when Finland was an autonomous province of Russia. Early on the factory grew so large that a town named Nokia was established for its workforce. It still exists although the company no longer has a presence there.

Diversifying into electrical power production, Nokia found a major customer in the Finnish Rubber Works, which became the country's major manufacturer of rubber products such as galoshes and raincoats. Following the 1918 Russian Revolution Finland fell into civil war but eventually gained independence, losing its vital Russian markets in the process. Nokia's early commitment to innovation and diversification has to be seen in the context of the political dangers the country faced as well as the difficulty in competing with major Western conglomerates. To survive, Finnish businesses had to co-operate with one another and accept the close involvement of the state. Nokia formed a "coalition" with two partners: its customer, the Finnish Rubber Works and the fast-growing Finnish Cable Works which supplied the booming telephone and electricity industries.

The three companies, each leaders in their respective markets, managed to grow during the Great Depression and merger talks began.

The Second World War was devastating for Finland, which fought first the Russians and then the Germans. Once the Cold War had set in, the country found itself in a very delicate position, having to foster a far closer relationship with USSR than the West approved of. The country did not receive US aid for post-war reconstruction, had to pay heavy war reparations to Russia and had difficulty in trading with the West because of fears that any new technology it was given would be passed to Russia (concerns that "Finlandization" would spread became a bugbear of the Western powers). The cable business benefited, however, by becoming a major supplier of cable to Russia. The company began to diversify into electronics, another industry with a bright future.

In 1967 the three partner firms finally merged in an uncomfortable deal that was intended to lessen the power of the banks which financed them. With the paper business maturing (it had grown massively in the preceding 70 years) and the rubber business shrinking, it was not clear that there would be synergy benefits from the merger.

The company managed to balance its exports between East and West. Survival in a deeply politicized economy meant constantly searching for new growth markets and new ways of doing more with limited financial resources. Students of the company claim that Nokia has had an unusually high degree of willingness to move into new businesses and to add value wherever possible, from technology right through to design and marketing.

Although electronics was a tiny part of the company in the 1960s, their research was cutting edge – the company was working in semiconductors and developed its own telephony products, including a radio telephone (1963), a modem (1965) and their first telecoms success, the DX 2000, a digital switch which has developed into its current mobile network infrastructure. By the early 1980s, Nokia was heavily involved in early mobile phone technology, including pagers. Its electronics division had also grown substantially in other areas, notably TV manufacturing and IT.

Nokia's big break in mobile telephony was when the GSM standard[4] was introduced in the late 1980s and the company began to supply GSM networks to companies in other countries. As the USSR collapsed at the end of the decade, Finland was thrown into an economic crisis and sought closer ties to the European Union, joining in 1993. In embracing the free market philosophy, the changes in the country allowed Nokia to make a major play for control of the global mobile market, raising finance in major international stock markets and moving faster than the sluggish telephone utilities elsewhere, many of which were reluctant to face up to the loss of their monopolies that came with privatization and deregulation.

By the end of the 1990s, Nokia was one of the three major mobile phone manufacturers in the world. In 1998 its market capitalization trebled to $250bn. Few expected mobile telephony to grow as fast as it has – the global market for handsets alone was worth $40bn in 1998 and is forecast to double by 2003. In many developing countries, such as China, people have leapfrogged from no phone to mobile phone because of the lack of availability of land lines. Mass markets have developed everywhere as people have discovered the joys of constant communication. In 2000, a staggering 200 million people acquired a hand phone. Annual unit sales may reach one billion by 2006. With such rapid growth, current perceived problems are to do with supply – analysts worry about component shortages and late introduction of new products. Growth in demand, we are assured, will not be a problem for many years to come.

KEY INSIGHTS

» Nokia's current success did not come easily or quickly. The company's electronics division is said to have lost money for almost two decades. Its willingness to persevere has much to do with Finland's difficult political circumstances in the past. The drive to find ways to prosper was arguably much greater for Finnish companies than for its more comfortable rivals in Western countries – for Nokia, necessity has indeed been the mother of invention.

» Although growth in mobile telephony looks bright, increased competition puts pressure on the current market leaders. At some point in the future the company will have to look for new industries to enter. Its track record of boldness suggests that it may succeed in finding fresh ways to add value.

» Industry watchers point to other factors contributing to Nokia's remarkable achievements, such as good customer relationships, a flat organization and good co-operation at board level. Others argue that these are dwarfed by the power of being in the right place at the right time. The much-touted "first mover advantage" may not always be the benefit it is claimed to be, but in an industry that was long due for reform Nokia's lean and audacious organization has so far been able to outshine its competitors.

TIMELINE FOR NOKIA

» **1865**: Nokia founded as a paper and pulp mill.
» **1917**: Nokia becomes part of a three-company alliance in the paper, rubber, power and cable industries.
» **1967**: The three companies finally merge.
» **1970s**: The company moves heavily into electronics.
» **1993**: Nokia is the first hand phone maker to produce products that function on all existing digital systems.
» **1999**: Nokia captures the lion's share of global profits on hand phones (70%).

NOTES

1 Quoted in an unpublished article by Stephen J. Simurda, "The Global Murdoch", www.umass.edu/journal/faculty/steve/unpubar-ticles/murdoch.html

2 Gough, L. (2001) *Investing in Biotechnology Stocks*, John Wiley, Singapore.

3 Gough, L. (2001) *Investing in Biotechnology Stocks*, John Wiley, Singapore.
4 GSM used to stand for Groupe Speciale Mobile, who developed the standard, and now stands for Global System for Mobile Communications.

Key Concepts

This chapter provides a glossary of accounting terms and discusses important ideas relating to value, such as:

» intellectual capital;
» value-based management (VBM);
» the Balanced Scorecard;
» calculating discounted cash flow, net present value, internal rate of return;
» valuing listed companies.

"Forecasting is not a respectable intellectual activity, and not worthwhile beyond the shortest of periods."

Peter Drucker, management guru[1]

GLOSSARY

Accounting policies – Those principles and practices applied by an entity that specify how the effects of transactions and other events are to be reflected in the accounts. For example, an entity may have a policy of revaluing fixed assets or of maintaining them at historical cost. Accounting policies do not include estimation techniques.

Accounts payable – American terminology for creditors.

Accounts receivable – American terminology for debtors.

Accrual – An expense or a proportion thereof not invoiced prior to the balance sheet date but included in the accounts sometimes on an estimated basis.

Accruals concept – Income and expenses are recognized in the period in which they are earned or incurred, rather than the period in which they happen to be received or paid.

Asset – Any property or rights owned by the company that have a monetary value. In UK accounting standards, assets are defined as "rights or other access to future economic benefits controlled by an entity as a result of past transactions or events."

Balance sheet – A statement describing what a business owns and owes at a particular date.

Break-even analysis – A form of analysis that relates activity to totals of revenue and costs based on the classification of costs into fixed and variable.

Break-even point – The level of activity at which the fixed costs of a project are just covered by the contribution from sales. At this point there is neither a profit nor a loss.

Capital employed – The aggregate amount of long-term funds invested in or lent to the business and used by it in carrying out its operations.

Cashflow forecast – A statement of future, anticipated cash balances based on estimated cash inflows and outflows over a given period.

Cashflow statement – A statement of cashflows during the most recent accounting period. The required format for a cashflow statement is laid down in accounting standards.

Comparability – The requirement that once an accounting policy for a particular item in the accounts has been adopted, the same policy should be used from one period to the next. Any change in policy must be fully disclosed. Comparability is also important when comparing entities in the same industry. They should, wherever possible, use similar accounting policies.

Contingent liability – A possible obligation arising from past events whose existence will be confirmed only by the occurrence of one or more uncertain future events not wholly within the entity's control.

Costs of capital – The weighted average costs of funds to a company based on the mix of equity and loan capital and their respective costs. This is sometimes used as the required rate of return in a discounted cashflow.

Costs of goods sold (or cost of sales) – Those costs (usually raw materials, labor, and production overheads) directly attributable to goods that have been sold. The difference between sales and cost of goods sold is gross profit.

Creditors – Amounts due to those who have supplied goods or services to the business.

Current asset – An asset which, if not already in cash form, is expected to be converted into cash within 12 months of the balance sheet date.

Current cost – The convention by which assets are valued at the cost of replacement at the balance sheet date (net of depreciation for fixed assets).

Current liability – An amount owed which will have to be paid within 12 months of the balance sheet date.

Current ratio – The ratio of current assets to current liabilities in a balance sheet, providing a measure of business liquidity.

Debentures – Long-term loans, usually secured on the company's assets.

Debtors – Amounts due from customers to whom goods or services have been sold but for which they have not yet paid.

Deferred asset/liability – An amount receivable or payable more than 12 months after the balance sheet date.

Deferred taxation – An estimate of a tax liability payable at some estimated future date, resulting from timing differences in the taxation and accounting treatment of certain items of income and expenditure.

Depreciation – An estimate of the proportion of the cost of a fixed asset which has been consumed (whether through use, obsolescence, or the passage of time) during the accounting period.

Discounted cashflow (DCF) – A method of appraisal for investment projects. The total incremental stream of cash for a project is tested to assess the level of return it delivers to the investor. If the return exceeds the required, or hurdle, rate the project is recommended on financial terms or vice versa.

Distribution – The amount distributed to shareholders out of the profits of the company, usually in the form of a cash dividend.

Dividend cover – The ratio of the amount of profit reported for the year to the amount distributed.

Dividend yield – The ratio of the amount of dividend per share to the market share price of a listed company.

Earnings per share – The amount of profit (after tax and any extraordinary items) attributable to shareholders divided by the number of ordinary shares in issue.

EBIT – Earnings (profit) before interest and tax.

EBITDA – Earnings (profit) before interest, tax, depreciation and amortization. This measure of operating cashflow is considered to be an important measure of the performance of an entity.

Estimation techniques – The methods adopted by an entity to arrive at estimated monetary amounts for items in the accounts. For example, of the various methods that could be adopted for depreciation, the entity may select to depreciate using the straight-line method.

Exceptional item – Income or expenditure that, although arising from the ordinary course of business, is of such unusual size or incidence that it needs to be disclosed separately.

Expense – A cost incurred, or a proportion of a cost, the benefit of which is wholly used up in the earning of the revenue for a particular accounting period.

Extraordinary item - Material income or expenditure arising from outside the ordinary course of business. As a result of recent changes to accounting standards, it is considered that extraordinary items are extremely rare if not non-existent.

Fixed asset - Asset held for use by the business rather than for sale.

Fixed cost - A cost that does not vary in proportion to changes in the scale of operations, e.g. rent.

Gearing - Gearing is the word used to describe the financing of the company in terms of the proportion of capital provided by shareholders (equity) compared with the proportion provided by loan capital (debt).

Gearing ratios - There are many different ways to measure gearing. The commonest is probably the ratio of debt to equity. That is the ratio of long-term loans to shareholders' funds (which can be measured in terms of nominal value or market value). Another common approach (called the capital gearing ratio) is to calculate the percentage of debt to total capital (debt plus equity). The income gearing ratio is the ratio of interest payable to the profits out of which interest is paid.

Gross profit - The difference between sales and the cost of goods sold.

Historic cost convention - The convention by which assets are valued on the basis of the original cost of acquiring or producing them.

Hurdle rate - The rate of return decided on by a company as the minimum acceptable for capital investment. It will be governed by the company's cost of capital and it may allow for different levels of risk.

Interest cover - The relationship between the amount of profit (before interest and before tax) and the amount of interest payable during a period.

Internal rate of return (IRR) - The rate of discount that brings the present value of all the cashflows associated with a capital investment to zero. It measures the effective yield on the investment. If this yield is greater than the hurdle rate the investment is seen to be financially desirable and vice versa.

Liability – An amount owed. In UK accounting standards, liabilities are defined as "an entity's obligations to transfer economic benefits as a result of past transactions or events."

Liquidity – A term used to describe the cash resources of a business and its ability to meet its short-term obligations.

Listed investments – Those investments for which the market price is quoted on a recognized stock exchange. They may therefore be traded on that exchange.

Long-term liability – An amount payable more than 12 months after the balance sheet date.

Market price – The price of a quoted security for dealing in the open market.

Net assets – The amount of total assets less total liabilities.

Net book value – The cost (or valuation) of fixed assets less accumulated depreciation to date. Net book value bears no relationship to market value.

Net current assets – The amount of current assets less current liabilities.

Net present value (NPV) – A positive or negative value arrived at by discounting the cashflow from a capital project by the desired rate of return. If the value is positive, it means that the project is desirable and vice versa.

Net realizable value – An amount at which an asset could be sold in its existing condition at the balance sheet date, after deducting any costs to be incurred in disposing of it.

Nominal value – The face value of a share or other security.

Opportunity cost – The alternative advantage foregone as a result of the commitment of resources to one particular end.

Overhead – Any expense, other than the direct cost of materials or labor, involved in making a company's products.

Payback period – A term used in investment appraisal. It refers to the time required for the non-discounted cash inflow to accumulate to the initial cash outflow in the investment.

Prepayment – The part of a cost which is carried forward as an asset in the balance sheet to be recognized as an expense in the ensuing period(s) in which the benefit will be derived from it, e.g. the payment in advance of rates.

Price/earnings ratio – The relationship between the market price of a share and its latest reported earnings per share.

Profit – The difference between the revenues earned in the period and the costs incurred in earning them. Alternative definitions are possible according to whether the figure is struck before or after tax.

Profit and loss account – A statement summarizing the revenues and the costs incurred in earning them during an accounting period.

Provision – A liability of uncertain timing or amount. A provision should only be recognized in the balance sheet when an entity has a present obligation (legal or constructive) as a result of a past event. It is probable that a transfer of economic benefits will be required to settle the obligation, and a reliable estimate can be made of the amount of the obligation. Unless these conditions are met, no provision should be recognized.

Quick ratio – The ratio of those current assets readily convertible into cash (usually current assets less stock) to current liabilities.

Residual value – A notional cash inflow attributed to a capital project to allow for value remaining in the project at the final year of the assessment.

Revaluation reserve – The increase in value of a fixed asset as a result of a revaluation. This needs to be included in the balance sheet as part of shareholders' funds in order to make the balance sheet balance.

Revenue – Money received from selling the product of the business.

Revenue reserves – The accumulated amount of profit less losses generated by the company since its incorporation and retained in it. It is usually called "profit and loss account" in the balance sheet.

Sensitivity analysis – Analysis of the change in the output values of an equation by small changes to the input values; it is used to assess the risk in an investment project.

Share capital – Stated in the balance sheet at its nominal value and (if fully paid, and not subject to any share premium) representing the amount of money introduced into the company by its shareholders at the time the shares were issued.

Shareholders' funds – A measure of the shareholders' total interest in the company, represented by the total of share capital plus reserves.

Share premium – The surplus over and above nominal value received in consideration for the issue of shares.

Turnover – Revenue from sales.

Variable cost – A cost that increases or decreases in line with changes in the level of activity.

Working capital – Current assets less current liabilities, representing the amount a business needs to invest and which is continually circulating in order to finance its stock, debtors, and work in progress.

Work in progress – Goods (or services) in the course of production (or provision) at the balance sheet date.

INTELLECTUAL CAPITAL MANAGEMENT

From the early 1960s economic researchers have been investigating the efficient use of resources as an approach to business strategy. Companies have different, often unique, intellectual resources that are not easily changed – specialized skills and know-how cannot be bought in the short term.

Management guru Peter Drucker has argued that knowledge has become a more important business resource than labor or capital: "Value is now created by 'productivity' and 'innovation,' both applications of knowledge, to work." Drucker says that "knowledge workers" are now more than a third of the workforce and are increasing in power – they "own their knowledge and can take it with them wherever they go."

Knowledge-based industries are now the leaders of the world economy, whether they are manufacturers (IT hardware, pharmaceuticals) or service providers (the media and entertainment industries). Recognizing these facts, knowledge management has become something of a fad, with a proliferation of conferences and proprietary approaches to measuring and exploiting a company's "knowledge capital." Large companies dependent on knowledge workers have a vital need to ensure that as much knowledge as possible is passed on to other employees, and there have been successful initiatives in this area by firms such as Hewlett Packard.

Much that is written about intellectual capital is very plainly selling snake oil. There is nothing at all new about the need for training or the opportunities and dangers associated with dependence on highly skilled personnel. The issue has become more important in recent years because of the change from blue-collar to white-collar working in the developed world as processes become more automated and manufacturing shifts to countries with cheaper labor. Not all organizations have the valuable intellectual capital necessary to become the next Microsoft or Genentech, yet there are plenty of advisors eager to sell them consultancy in this field. Nevertheless, the extraordinary power wielded by companies with unique skills in growth industries such as IT does demand attention. Managing talented employees often requires allowing a flexible, informal environment that fosters creativity, as has notably occurred in Silicon Valley where handfuls of eccentric, jeans-wearing software developers working strange hours in small teams have created more value than multitudes of disciplined 9–5 office workers elsewhere.

Valuing intellectual capital requires the ability to measure it. A number of Scandinavian firms have pioneered the field, producing indices and ratios to present a complete view of a company's intellectual assets. Skandia AFS, for example, publishes these measures in its annual report. It attempts to distinguish between "human capital" that employees take home with them and "structural capital" that remains at the office permanently, such as patents, databases and customer relationships.

In Japan, where the first important work on knowledge management originally appeared (*Mobilizing Invisible Assets* by Hiroyuki Itami[2]) there is greater awareness of the distinction between explicit knowledge that can be formally transferred between employees and tacit knowledge that exists within individuals and is the primary source of the creation of new knowledge. Tacit knowledge, say the Japanese, is subtle and can only be fostered through a company culture of willing participation. A talented knowledge worker will not be eager to "transfer" knowledge to a company that may then be prepared to dispense with his or her services.

The current position is that while valiant attempts are being made to find ways of valuing "wetware" (the knowledge in people's heads), no satisfactory universal system has yet been established.

VALUE-BASED MANAGEMENT (VBM)

Under pressure from institutional investors, companies everywhere have turned to value creation as an overtly stated objective. In the

USA, the Securities & Exchange Commission (SEC) requires companies to report value creation in their statements. The Boston Consulting Group (BCG) agrees with other pundits in stressing the importance of finding ways of measuring value creation. BCG promotes the use of total shareholder return (TSR) as the ultimate yardstick. TSR is the total amount received by investors from their stock, including dividends and final sales, less the purchase price. As we saw in Chapter 3, companies are often subject to stock price fluctuations beyond their control, so TSR has to be put in context by comparing it with the TSR of similar companies, the sector as a whole and the overall market. This allows analysts to adjust for influences that move the industry or the market, such as interest rate changes and economic shocks.

BCG has argued that there is no single method for achieving outstanding performance, but that nevertheless outperforming the average is desirable. This is problematic, since by definition the majority cannot outperform the average – if all companies performed extremely well, the average would simply move up to reflect the change.

A key point in creating value is that it does not necessarily require growth. A company's growth may slow while it increases profitability and thus its value to the shareholders. Ways to drive up value vary in different businesses and, say BCG, value creation must be tailor-made to fit the particular firm, based on accurate measurement of its cost of capital, growth, profits and cash flow. The best opportunities for creating value are at the operating level, where managers are often pursuing the wrong performance measures. By encouraging an awareness of TSR and the trade-offs between different drivers of value – i.e. the effect of sales growth on cash flow – companies can help managers to pull in the same direction. Many performance measures are known to cause people to make value-destroying decisions unwittingly; by relating everything back to TSR, this can be avoided.

THE BALANCED SCORECARD

The "Balanced Scorecard" was devised in the early 1990s by David Norton and Robert Kaplan[3] as a way of systematically gathering feedback from the business to steer company strategy. In addition to using traditional financial measures, it also employs measurement-based management and total quality management (TQM). Like TQM, the

Balanced Scorecard uses feedback from the outputs of internal business processes, but it also requires feedback from business outcomes. It terms this combination "double-loop feedback". As with other value-creation systems, the Balanced Scorecard aims to take into account the value of intellectual activity.

ARE EPPS REALLY BETTER PERFORMANCE MEASURES?

EVA, VBM and the Balanced Scorecard are categorized by academics as economic profit plans (EPPs). Taken as a whole, they are the most prominent system of rewarding managers today and have been widely adopted by blue chip companies such as Coca Cola, Monsanto and Eli Lilly. But are they really an improvement upon earlier reward schemes? If so, then companies using EPP should perform better than their competitors.

Craig Lewis of the Owen Business School at Vanderbilt University and Chris Hogan of Southern Methodist University decided to try to find out. Taking the four-year period after companies had instituted an EPP, Hogan and Lewis found that there was indeed significant performance improvement, with the median average return on assets (ROA) increasing from 3.5% to 4.7% over the period and the median ratio of operating income to total assets increasing from 15.8% to 16.7%. Testing with many standard accounting measures, the researchers describe EPP companies as realizing "dramatic long-run improvements in operating performance."

But is this success simply a function of a prosperous economy during the period examined? And do EPP firms do better than their rivals? The researchers chose non-EPP companies of similar size in the same industry that had similar operating performance as EPP firms prior to starting EPP and found no statistically significant difference between the two groups. They offer two possible explanations for this. Managers may have foreseen improving economic conditions and adopted EPP in order to improve their own bonuses; but it is also possible that all firms have made efforts to align managers' incentives with shareholders' interests in various ways (not only EPP) and that this has produced good results.

Hogan and Lewis looked at changes in operating performance and related them to "changes in the compensation, ownership, and governance structures of adopting and control firms" and found that the changes were similar across all the companies. For instance, bonuses increased by 39.1% in the year that companies started EPP, but in similar non-EPP firms bonuses increased by 37.4%. This, they say, "is not consistent" with the idea that managers took on EPP opportunistically, especially as it might well have been easier to improve bonuses using existing reward schemes.

Hogan and Lewis conclude that EPP is neither worse nor better than other reward schemes at increasing shareholder value.

EVALUATING INVESTMENTS: DISCOUNTED CASH FLOW (DCF) AND INTERNAL RATE OF RETURN (IRR)

Also known as "net present value analysis," the principle of DCF is to compare the present value of the total income from a project with the present value of the total costs involved. The difference between the two is the "net present value" (NPV) – if this is a positive figure, then the project is acceptable.

If there is a choice between several business investments, then the one with the highest NPV is normally the most desirable.

EXAMPLE 8.1

You have a choice between two business investments, both of which require an initial investment of 1 million dollars. All subsequent costs will be paid for out of income:

Project 1

Total cost $1mn
Estimated future net cash flow (after costs)
Year 1 $0.5mn
Year 2 $0.5mn
Year 3 $1.1mn
After Year 3   Zero

Project 2

Total cost $1mn
Estimated future net cash flow (after costs)
Year 1 $1mn
Year 2 $0.05mn
Year 3 $0.05mn
After Year 3   Zero

To calculate which project is the more valuable using DCF, you must now select the discount rate. For corporations, this is usually the cost of capital to the firm.

Assume that the company's cost of capital is 12%. Using widely available NPV tables, you then discount the incoming cash by the factor given. A 12% rate gives 0.893 for Year 1, 0.797 for Year 2 and 0.712 for Year 3. These factors adjust the value of the cash to its present value, by taking into account the time you will have to wait before you receive it.

Project 1

Present value of cash flow in $= (\$0.5\text{mn} \times 0.893)$

$+ (\$0.5\text{mn} \times 0.797) + (\$1.1\text{mn} \times 0.712)$

$= \$0.4465\text{mn} + \$0.3985\text{mn} + \$0.7832\text{mn}$

$= \$1,628,200$

Present value of total cost $= \$1$ mn
Note: if some of the investment costs are incurred in later years, they must be discounted at the same rate (in this case, 12%).

Net present value of cash flow minus cost

$= \$1,628,200 - \$1,000,000 = \$628,000$

Project 2

Present value of cash flow in $= (\$1mn \times 0.893)$

$+ (\$0.05mn \times 0.797) + (\$0.05mn \times 0.712)$

$= \$0.893mn + \$0.0396mn + \$0.0356mn$

$= \$0.9682mn$

Present value of total cost $= \$1mn$

Net present value of cash flow minus cost

$= \$968,200 - \$1,000,000 = (\$31,800)$

Comparing the two projects, we see that Project 2 has a negative NPV and is therefore unacceptable. Project 1 has a positive NPV of $628,000, so it will create value.

In practice, potential investments may have widely ranging cost and cash flow patterns which make them more complex to calculate, but the principle remains the same. Of more concern are the assumptions on which the DCF are based. Do we really know for sure that a given sum of money will arrive 15 years from now? Some businesses may be more certain than others, but there is still considerable risk involved. One way to adjust for this is to assign different discount rates according to the perceived risk. If Project 1 is quite risky, while Project 2 is not at all risky, then managers might assign a discount rate of 15% to Project 1, which would produce a lower NPV, while leaving Project 2's discount rate at the cost of capital, 12%.

One common mistake is to try to adjust for risk again, once the NPVs have been calculated. Suppose that Project 2's NPV was positive, but less than the NPV of Project 1. By discounting Project 1 at 15% you have already adjusted for its risk, so it would be an error to prefer Project 2 over Project 1. The risk assigned is only an estimate, however, and may be incorrect – a higher discount rate would produce a lower NPV.

INTERNAL RATE OF RETURN (IRR)

IRR is a concept related to DCF. It is the discount rate that will give you the expected compound annual rate of return on the investment, and is calculated by finding the rate that will make the NPV equal zero. This can be done by trial and error or with a computer program. Here's how it works:

EXAMPLE 8.2

Returning to Project 1 in Example 8.1, you might take a guess that the IRR is 20%. From NPV tables, you see that the factors are 0.833 for Year 1, 0.694 for Year 2 and 0.579 for Year 3.

Project 1 cash flow $= (\$0.5\text{mn} \times 0.833)$

$+ (\$0.5\text{mn} \times 0.694) + (\$1.1\text{mn} \times 0.579)$

$= \$0.4165\text{mn} + \$0.347\text{mn} + \$0.6369\text{mn}$

$= \$1, 400, 400$

Present value of total cost $= \$1\text{mn}$

Net present value of cash flow minus cost $= \$1, 400, 400$

$- \$1, 000, 000 = (\$400, 400)$

We are trying to make the NPV equal to zero, so we need to try a higher discount rate.

The correct IRR for Project 1 is approximately 41%, which brings the NPV very close to zero:

Project 1 cash flow $= (\$0.5\text{mn} \times 0.702)$

$+ (\$0.5\text{mn} \times 0.503) + (\$1.1\text{mn} \times 0.364)$

$= \$1, 002, 900$

Present value of total cost $= \$1\text{mn}$

Net present value of cash flow minus cost $= \$1, 002, 900$

$- \$1, 000, 000 = (\$2, 900)$

This NPV figure is close enough to zero, being a fraction of 1% of the total cost, to make 41% an acceptable rounding of the IRR.

NPV and IRR are usually equally good methods for deciding on whether or not an investment will deliver a desirable return. In some cases they can produce conflicting results and, in general, the NPV method is preferred because it is likely to point to the project that will add the most value. Sometimes, though, a low cost project will have a high IRR but a low NPV in comparison to the other options. Often firms will choose the low cost project because they regard it as the least risky investment.

VALUING LISTED COMPANIES

Investors in the common stocks (called "ordinary shares" in some countries) of companies expect to receive cash flows from dividend payouts and the sale of stock. Neither of these are predictable, but there are many models that attempt to estimate the intrinsic value of a stock by making assumptions about growth rates. If your estimate of the intrinsic value is higher than the current market price, then the stock is a buy and if it is lower, then it is considered to be overvalued.

One traditional model takes the view that the market price of a stock is dependent on the capacity of the company to pay dividends, and therefore uses a formula that calculates the present value of all future dividends. To do this, the model assumes that dividends will grow at a constant rate, and that this growth rate will be less than the capitalization rate. The capitalization rate is similar to the discount rate used in the NPV calculations above – it represents the relative riskiness of the type of company. One way of looking at the capitalization rate is to say that it is the minimum annual return that investors will accept, given the perceived risk.

The model uses the formula:

Present value = expected dividend at the end of the first year / (capitalization rate − expected dividend growth rate)

EXAMPLE 8.3

Suppose a company is predicted to pay a dividend of $2 per share this year. You expect dividends to grow on average by 6% annually in the future and you assess appropriate capitalization rate (risk) for this class of company to be 20%.

Using the formula, we get

Present value $= 2/(0.2 - 0.06)$

$= 2/0.14$

$= \$14.29$

The intrinsic value of the stock is $14.29.

This formula can be applied to more difficult situations. For instance, many companies do not currently pay dividends, so how can you value them? The answer is to forecast the point in the future when it will begin to pay dividends, apply the formula and then discount this back to the present. Similarly, if you expect a company to enjoy a period of high growth followed by a return to "normal" growth, you can use the formula to calculate the present value of the stock during each of the high growth years, add them together and then add the sum to the present value of the stock price at the end of the period.

DEPRECIATION

Accounting for depreciation has long been recognized as one of the classic problems with traditional accounting because, as with other aspects of accounting, it does not recognize the "time value" of money. For instance, payments due in the future are not discounted to their present value. This failure to discount can produce serious distortions.

Traditionally, differences between the net book value (the original cost of the asset minus the total of depreciation charged) and the actual market value are not shown in the accounts until the asset is sold. Perfect depreciation would mean that the asset's net book value would be exactly equal to the market value of the asset at any time during its useful life. Despite the numerous approaches to depreciation, this is rarely, if ever, achieved.

R&D efforts are increasingly being seen as assets. In contrast to fixed assets such as machinery, R&D assets tend to rise in value as time passes and discoveries are turned into income generating products and services. Some believe that one should apply "economic depreciation" to R&D assets, which may actually produce negative depreciation in the early years.

In practice, the depreciation method used for financial accounting is often different from the one required for tax purposes. For valuation, the best practice is to choose the depreciation method that most closely mimics the real-life rate of depreciation of the asset.

NOTES

1 Drucker, P.F. (1973) *Management: Tasks, Responsibilities, Practices*, Harper Business, New York.

2 Itami, H. with Roehl, T.W. (1987) *Mobilising Invisible Assets*, Harvard University Press, Cambridge.

3 Kaplan, R.S. and Norton, D.P. (1996) *The Balanced Scorecard*, Harvard Business School Press, Boston, MA.

Resources

A guide to useful Websites, books and journals on the following topics:

- » company information;
- » calculating values;
- » EVA;
- » the efficient market;
- » management consultancies;
- » patents;
- » intangibles;
- » financial research.

Management science has been a disappointment ... It would have been more prudent ... to speak of "management analysis" than "management sciences."

Peter Drucker, management guru[1]

Valuation is a vast subject covering many areas of specialization. The aim here is to give details of some of the key Websites and books to consult when starting out in this field. Websites often change their contents and addresses; the list of sites was accurate at the time of writing but may change. Use search engines such as Google (www.google.com) to find lost sites.

COMPANY INFORMATION: THE SECURITIES & EXCHANGE COMMISSION (SEC)

www.sec.gov

To value a firm properly, you cannot rely on second-hand data. The SEC's Website contains a vast database of statutory company filings (EDGAR) that cover all companies registered on the US stock exchange (this includes many foreign companies) and also private companies with more than 500 shareholders and $10mn in assets. The SEC is arguably the best regulator in the world; it certainly provides the most information for investors.

Among the most useful items available on EDGAR are:

» The financial statements – the annual report, 10Q, 10K and 8K forms, which give yearly and quarterly figures and amendments.
» Proxy statements – these are submitted annually, and show how many stocks are owned by the management, their salaries, employment contracts and perks, the major stockholders, any pending lawsuits and so on.
» 13-D, which gives details of any purchase of a controlling position in a company.
» Form 4, which key managers must submit within 10 days of any month in which they bought or sold their own company's stocks.
» Form 144, which key managers, not just the directors, must submit when they place an order to sell some of their own company's shares.

CALCULATING VALUES

www.stern.nyu.edu/~adamodar

As Warren Buffett likes to say, "And now, spinach time!" Calculation of value is hard work, but for those who are prepared to master its complexities, Professor Aswath Damodaran of New York University provides a rich resource at his Website.

Damodaran believes that DCF models make the best valuation tools, but he also provides detailed information on how to apply other valuation methods. DCF is best, he says, because cash flows are harder to manipulate than other accounting ratios such as EPS. Without DCF, the valuation process tends to become a matter of comparison between companies. If all the stocks compared are over-valued, then your valuation will be too high too, as we have seen in the recent Internet bubble. Damodaran points out that it is sell-side analysts – whose job it is to promote investments to others – who prefer relative valuation methods such as price-earnings and price-sales ratios that may be based on over-optimistic estimates of sales growth. Buy-side analysts in the same firms are often much more cautious and tend to prefer DCF.

The site has nine different DCF models in Excel spreadsheets and detailed explanations of how to estimate DCF inputs and the differences between the models. Damodaran points out that DCF does not provide any guarantees, and must be recalculated every time there is a significant event in the company's life, such as a drop in profits, the loss of a major client or a reverse in inflation or interest rates. According to this view the value of a company is ever-changing, often because of factors beyond the control of managers.

EVA

www.sternstewart.com

This is the Website of Stern Stewart, the consultancy whose partners, Joel Stern and Bennet Stewart, were the original authors of the economic value added (EVA) concept that is currently the most widely used approach to measuring and building shareholder value. Based on the idea of "economic profit" that has long been known to economists, EVA is both a performance measure for executive compensation and a way of focusing priorities at every level of a company.

The site provides introductory discussions of EVA and comparisons with other measures. It also publishes yearly performance rankings of major corporations in several countries based on market value added (MVA), the difference between the market capitalization of a firm and the total capital invested. A positive MVA figure indicates an increase in shareholder value.

The Website also promotes a book by Joel Stern and John S. Shiely with Irwin Ross, *The EVA Challenge: Implementing Value Added Change in an Organization*[2] that is worth reading and presents interesting case studies of the application of EVA ideas in the real world.

The success of EVA means that it is now big business and has inevitably attracted the scrutiny of academics. Criticism centers mainly around objections that EVA cannot be a universal panacea and that, like all measures, it can be misapplied. For instance, it has been suggested that companies with a high level of debt may benefit less from EVA because they may already be forced to run close to maximum efficiency.

THE BALANCED SCORECARD

www.rens.com

David Kaplan, co-creator of the Balanced Scorecard (see Chapter 8), has a Website for his consultancy firm, Renaissance Solutions, with useful information about this topic. Of interest if you are seeking an update on the latest developments are The Balanced Scorecard White Papers, which cover a wide range of issues on such matters as reforming operations and managing knowledge.

THE EFFICIENT MARKET

A Random Walk Down Wall Street

A Random Walk Down Wall Street, by Burton Malkiel,[3] is the best overview of the development of academic thinking about how stock prices move. It points out the problems with two popular investment theories, fundamental analysis (the idea that you can predict stock prices by analyzing intrinsic value) and technical analysis (the idea that you can predict stock prices by extrapolating from historical patterns of price movements). Malkiel explains the academic view that prices tend to move randomly around an overall long-term trend in the market and that stock picking is unlikely to be successful because the market is "efficient," meaning that all knowable information reaches professional investors at the same moment. The book is aimed at private investors, not business managers, so the focus is on advice – Malkiel concludes that tracking a major market index, which assures you of doing neither better nor worse than the average, is a more certain way of assuring acceptable returns in the long run than any other method.

Many professional investors do not believe that the market is efficient, or, at least, not all the time. For example, George Soros, the prominent hedge fund investor, seeks out situations across the globe where the market is in "disequilibrium" and prices of stocks, bonds and currencies are clearly out of whack. Nor does Warren Buffett accept market efficiency; he believes that people misjudge companies and therefore misjudge prices. Whatever the truth, for the small investor, and the majority of professionals, following the market average is likely to produce better results (remember, the majority of investment professionals underperform the market).

MANAGEMENT CONSULTANCIES: MCKINSEY, MERCER AND AT KEARNEY

www.mckinsey.com

www.mercermc.com

www.atkearney.com

With so many management consultancies vying for attention on the Web, it is not always easy to choose where to invest your time. These three notable firms offer useful downloadable reports and articles of relevance to valuation and value management. At the time of writing, for instance, AT Kearney has a number of well-written reports on the future of e-commerce and mobile commerce. McKinsey's Website reproduces articles and executive summaries from its journal, the *McKinsey Quarterly*, which despite its self-promotional bias remains an excellent source for current management thinking. Mercer's heavy emphasis on growth provides much useful information for the student of value.

PREDICTION AND FORECASTING

www.seattle.battelle.org/services/e&s/foresite/in-dex.htm

In spite of our inability to predict the future accurately, efforts continue to look for ways of preparing better for possible outcomes. One line of attack is scenario planning, used by many groups in different fields, not only business. The report at the Website above was produced by the Battelle Seattle Research Center in 1997 for the US Department of Energy. It surveys a number of scenario planning projects from a wide range of organizations, including:

» Shell Oil;
» Fraunhofer Institute for Systems and Innovation Research, Germany;
» National Institute of Science and Technology Policy, Japan;
» US Army Environmental Policy Institute;
» Australian Science and Technology Council.

The jargon term for forecasting activities is "foresighting," which better conveys the lack of certainty inherent in this field. The report argues that foresighting helps organizations to think creatively about the future and thereby become able to adapt quickly to external change.

INTANGIBLES

www.brookings.edu/es/research/projects/intangibles/intangibles.htm

Published by the Brookings Institution's Economic Studies program this Website aims to promote debate on approaches to the measurement and reporting of intangibles and contains useful long summaries of two reports, *The Intangible Capital Report* by Baruch Lev and *The Unseen Wealth Report*. Baruch Lev is professor of accounting and finance at New York University's Stern School of Business and a prominent figure in the intangibles field (see Chapter 2). His report looks at trends, existing practices, decision-making processes, the institutional environment and economic theory relating to intangibles. *The Unseen Wealth Report* examines tax policies, intellectual property, R&D policy, the SEC and financial reporting and human capital.

PATENTS

www.uspto.gov

www.oreillynet.com/patents

Patents with existing commercial applications are among the more easily valued types of knowledge capital because they have a limited life and can be directly associated with specific products generating measurable income streams. Today, the majority of patents go to corporations, not individuals or academic institutions. The US is the key territory for patents because of the value of its internal market, so the United States Patent and Trademark Office at www.uspto.gov is the first site to visit when exploring this complex area.

Technology publisher O'Reilly has a good section on patents called the Patents DevCenter at www.oreillynet.com/patents.

KNOWLEDGE MANAGEMENT LINKS

www.brint.com/OrgLrng.htm

You can find comprehensive links and lists of publications about knowledge management at this Website from Business Researcher's Interests. This massive site provides an impressive amount of information for the serious researcher.

THE INTANGIBLE ASSETS MONITOR

www.sveiby.com.au/IntangAss/CompanyMonitor.html

Karl-Erik Sveiby is another leading thinker on intellectual capital and helped to establish the non-financial measures used extensively by various Swedish companies (see Chapter 2). While not very attractively presented, this Website contains useful, well-documented information about his methods and those of others in the field.

WILLAMETTE MANAGEMENT ASSOCIATES

www.willamette.com/pubs/insights/99/Summer-99.html

This consulting and financial advisory company in Chicago publishes a number of in-depth articles about intellectual property on its site, covering important – and potentially measurable – areas such as copyrights and computer software. Extremely useful for the financially minded, it focuses on economic analysis rather than management rhetoric.

KNOWLEDGE MANAGEMENT AND ROI

www.harvardcomputing.com

An interesting report on how to measure the return on investment (ROI) of knowledge management systems before they are implemented is available at this site, providing specific guidance on ways of measuring the savings made and costs incurred. Published by the Harvard Computing Group, a business technology consultancy, it emphasizes the need to convince managers and other employees of the value of knowledge management and argues that logical measures are persuasive in this regard.

FINANCIAL EDUCATION AND RESEARCH

www.ssrn.com – Financial Economics Network (FEN)

www.finweb.com – FINWeb

www.finance.wat.ch – Finance Watch

These are three virtual library/link sites. The first, FEN, is the most scholarly and focuses on money management, investment banking, research services and journals and associations. FINWeb is managed by Professor James R. Garven at the University of Texas at Austin, and has useful links to archives of financial journals. Finance Watch is similar, providing a fairly comprehensive picture of all the serious financial information available on the Internet.

SHAREHOLDER VALUE MAGAZINE

www.kennedyinfo.com/ir/svm/svm.html

A useful magazine available online, covering the hot issues of the moment.

FURTHER READING

Armitrage, H.M. (1996) "Economic Value Creation: What Every Management Accountant Should Know," *Chartered Management Accountant: The Management Accounting Magazine*, 70 (Issue 8), 21ff.

Bacidore, J.M., Boquist, J.A., Milbourn, T.T. and Thakor, A.V. (1997) "The Search for the Best Financial Performance Measure," *Financial Analysts Journal* (May/June), 11-20.

Birchard, B. (1994) "Mastering the New Metrics", *Chief Financial Officer* (October).

Blair, A. (1997) "EVA Fever," *Management Today* (January), 42.

Blair, A. (1997) "Watching the New Metrics," *Management Today* (April).

Biddle, G., Bowen, R. and Wallace, J. (1997) "Evidence on the Relative and Incremental Information Content of EVA, Residual Income, Earnings and Operating Cash Flow," Working Paper, University of Washington.

Brossy, R. and Balkcom, J.E. (1994) "Getting Executives to Create Value", *Journal of Business Strategy*, 15, 18-21.

Copeland, T., Koller, T. and Murrin, J. (1994) *Valuation: Measuring and Managing the Value of Companies*, 2nd edn, John Wiley & Sons, New York.

Dillon, R.D. and Owers, J.E. (1997) "EVA as a Financial Metric: Attributes, Utilization, and Relationship to NPV," *Financial Practice and Education* (Spring/Summer), 32-40.

Ehrbar, A. (1998) *EVA: The Real Key to Creating Wealth*, John Wiley & Sons, New York.

Gough, L. (1999) *Trading the World's Markets*, John Wiley, Singapore.

Gough, L. (2001) *Investing in Biotechnology Stocks*, John Wiley, Singapore.

Grant, J.L. (1996) "Foundations of EVA for Investment Managers," *Journal of Portfolio Management*, Fall, 41.

Jones, T.P. (1995) "The Economic Value-added Approach to Corporate Investment," in *Corporate Financial Decision Making and Equity Analysis*, Institute of Chartered Financial Analysts Continuing Education, Association for Investment Management and Research, 21–30.

Padgett, T. (1997) "Hot New Evaluative Tool Winning Wall St. Adherents," *The American Banker*, March 14.

Kay, J. (1995) *Why Firms Succeed*, Oxford University Press, New York.

Madden, B.J. (1995) "The Case for Cash Flow ROI in Linking Company Performance with Market Valuation," Valuation Issues (November), 4–7.

Malkiel, B.G. (1990) *A Random Walk Down Wall Street*, Norton, New York.

Oliver, J. (1996) "Which Numbers Count," *Management Today* (November).

Peterson, P.P. and Peterson, D.R. (1996) *Company Performance and Measures of Value Added*, The Research Foundation of the Institute of Chartered Financial Analysts.

Saint, D.K. (1995) "Why Economic Value is a Yardstick for Numbers, Not People", *Financial Executive* (March/April), 9–11.

Sheehan, T.J. (1994) "To EVA or Not to EVA: Is That the Question?" *Journal of Applied Corporate Finance*, 7 (No. 2), 84–7.

Shiely, J.S. (1996) "Is Value Management the Answer?," *Chief Executive*, No. 119 (December), 54.

Stern, J. (1994) "No Incentive for Bad Management," *Corporate Finance* (March), 43–4.

Stern, J. and Shiely, J.S. with Ross, I. (2000) *The EVA Challenge: Implementing Value Added Change in an Organization*, John Wiley, New York.

Stewart, G.B. III (1991) *The Quest for Value*, HarperCollins, New York.

Thomas, R. and Edwards, L. (1993) "For Good Decisions, Determine Business Values More Accurately", *Corporate CashFlow* (September), 37–40.

Uyemura, D.G. (1997) "EVA: a Top-Down Approach to Risk Management," *The Journal of Lending & Credit Risk Management*, 79 (No. 6), 40.

Wallace, J. (1997) "Adopting Residual Income-Based Compensation Plans: Evidence of Effects on Management Actions," Working Paper, University of California, Irvine.

NOTES

1 Drucker, P.F. (1973) *Management: Tasks, Responsibilities, Practices*, Harper Business, New York.

2 Stern, J. and Shiely, J.S. with Ross, I. (2000) *The EVA Challenge: Implementing Value Added Change in an Organization*, John Wiley, New York.

3 Malkiel, B.G. (1990) *A Random Walk Down Wall Street*, Norton, New York.

Ten Steps to Making Valuation Work

Key points to remember in valuation and value enhancement, including:

- » unpredictability;
- » cash flows – the virtue of DCF;
- » performance measures – the pros and cons;
- » value enhancement – small improvements;
- » value enhancement – creating major competitive advantages.

In the 1960s, when Britain was plagued by balance-of-payments problems, a journalist asked the Chancellor of the Exchequer why the nation had fared so much better in the days of Queen Victoria. "Ah," he replied, "back then, we didn't have any statistics."

Paul Krugman, economist[1]

Valuation is not an exact science, in spite of all the efforts to make it so, because it is subject to constant change. To understand why, think about purchasing a house. The price you pay will be related to prices paid recently for similar properties in the area, but it is unlikely that you will pay exactly the same; you might, for instance, be willing to pay 10% more than another purchaser because it is your dream house or it is perfectly situated for travelling to your work. When you come to sell the house, the market is likely to have changed – you cannot know for certain exactly what price you can command at any given point in the future. To see the use of DCF, extend the analogy by thinking of purchasing a house for rental. Again, you cannot be certain of the rents you can obtain, but by study you can make educated guesses about the current rent and its growth over the coming years, and discount these back. This will not produce precisely accurate figures, but it will help you to decide, for instance, whether the cash flow from rent will cover your borrowing and maintenance costs.

Pressures on large public corporations are great and there is a natural tendency for people to make confident claims about value where no absolute certainty exists. Don't be deceived – valuation techniques are tools for decision-making in a complex and ever-changing world, not 100% guarantees of future outcomes.

In this chapter we will look at 10 key areas to bear in mind when considering any valuation question.

1. INVESTORS AND MANAGERS

Investors and managers need each other but while both want good returns, their options differ. Investors can take their money out of a company and invest elsewhere, so they are constantly comparing the performance of their investments with that of others. Since they have little or no direct influence over their investments, they have to rely principally on published information to assess value. If the figures in the annual report are manipulated, unsophisticated investors may be deceived, at least in the short term.

Managers' preoccupations are necessarily different. They must focus on one company at a time – although this can be for a short time, given managers' propensity to switch firms – and have a far more intimate knowledge of their business.

Both groups are subject to the temptation of trying to make a quick buck that may ultimately destroy value. Achieving sustainable profit growth over many years entails commitment and discipline – but also communication between the two parties. Managers can convince shareholders of their integrity and commitment, but only over time.

2. UNPREDICTABILITY

Human beings instinctively want certainty about the future, yet it is one thing that we certainly cannot have. For example, systematized strategic planning was once hailed as the last word on controlling future events. The Planning-Programming-Budgeting System (PPBS) was introduced by the US government in the 1960s and adopted by other nations, but by the 1980s it was widely recognized as having wholly failed to improve performance.

Economic forecasting has been equally unsuccessful; a study by Victor Zarnowitz,[2] an academic at the University of Chicago, found that leading forecasters had failed to predict accurately the quarterly US GNP growth in the early 1970s, for instance, while other studies show that forecasters have been unable to predict economic turning points through the last three decades any better than a "naïve forecast" that there would be no change.

We ignore unpredictability at our peril. If creating value becomes an entirely prescriptive set of rules, the results may well be disappointing. Lucky breaks, such as Microsoft's sale of MS-DOS to IBM, cannot be predicted, yet they may transform the fortunes of a company.

Companies need to be responsive to external change if they are to profit from it. We need to plan how to create value, but we have to be willing to revise our ideas in the face of new evidence. Strategizing for survival in a variety of potential economic circumstances is essential if a company is to create sustainable growth.

Recognizing unpredictability is a crucial attitude in successful valuation techniques. Sophisticated investors use DCF to estimate future income, but they recognize that these are only estimates and are not written in stone. Risk management techniques such as diversification and allowing for a large margin for error help to cushion companies and investors from unpleasant surprises.

3. CASHFLOWS

Hard-bitten professional investors and lenders have known for many years that DCF is the most realistic way to estimate value in most situations. It is unsafe to rely on other people's figures, however. DCF relies on estimates and assumptions, so to satisfy yourself of their realism you need to work through them yourself. Without being fully aware of what assumptions you have made, you will not be able to gauge whether or not things are progressing according to plan. The reliability of sales forecasts, upon which DCF principally depends, varies greatly; only an intimate knowledge of a company and its industry will enable you to judge, and even then there may be surprises.

4. KNOWLEDGE CAPITAL

The values of patents, brands and copyrights are possible to measure by relating them to cash flows already generated by products with which they are associated. For example, Disney cartoon characters have measurable value because of the movies, TV shows, books and merchandise that they help sell. More value can be squeezed out of "old" characters by associating them with new ones or selling existing products in new media. A cartoon character on the drawing board, or a patent for a product that has not come to market, may be much harder to value because there is no track record. The same intellectual asset may acquire enormous value simply by being acquired by a company with established distribution channels – the cartoon character designed by an independent artist is worthless unless it is purchased by a company such as Disney.

While systematizing and exploiting the knowledge inside the heads of company staff may be vital in specialized industries, it is often difficult for outsiders to gauge their true worth. In the biotechnology industry there have been frequent disappointments as promising therapies have failed to deliver results and it is clear that most external investors had no good way of estimating the likelihood of success.

Not everyone is in a knowledge business. You know if you really are. Ultimately the value of the knowledge in your firm will be tested in the market place. While investors are keen to get in early on promising products, they feel cheated by failure. Owners of valuable intellectual assets need to communicate the risks clearly if they are to sustain investment confidence.

5. VALUATION GLOBALLY

The globalization process is far from complete, and may never be so. Some theorists argue that globalization is best seen as the swing of a long-term economic pendulum and that the process may well reverse in the future. There is no good reason to be certain that 50 years from now we will be enjoying a utopian world of free capital flows and universal accounting standards. Globalization depends upon the political will of nation states. Countries are capable of closing their doors if they perceive a threat, as they have done frequently in the past.

Cross-border business is never easy. Differences in conditions across countries abound, and it is easy to miscalculate if you judge a foreign business by your own domestic standards. There is no substitute for an intimate knowledge of the local situation, not only of the industry but also of the specific political and regulatory risks in the country concerned. Many nations are somewhat schizophrenic in their attitudes; on the one hand they want foreign investment, but on the other they want to protect their own employees. For example, despite the EU's aspirations to allow freedom of movement for employees across the member states, countries still place subtle restrictions to inhibit this – it is not easy for, say, a British doctor to practice medicine in France. Marks & Spencer, a troubled British retailer, recently attracted violent criticism in France for closing down its operations there, an action that might have been applauded in a more shareholder-friendly country.

Some industries, such as pharmaceuticals, are more naturally suited to international business, having high barriers to entry and products that are universally in demand. The keys to any international valuation issue is to maximize information and to adopt risk reduction strategies; there can be few absolute certainties, especially in the long term.

6. THE DIFFERENCE BETWEEN REPORTED ACCOUNTS AND MANAGEMENT ACCOUNTS

People have known for many years that the accounts you find in annual reports can be misleading, not only because they can be deliberately massaged but also, and more importantly, because of accounting rules and practices that distort the true picture. Management accounting developed as an internal financial information system to help decision makers to see exactly what is happening in their businesses and take appropriate action. Today, with investors becoming increasingly sophisticated and demanding, the pressure is on to provide better information to outsiders to assist them in assessing the true value of a firm. This is particularly important in new knowledge-based industries where growth can be very rapid. For example, a small silicon chip maker (such as the UK firm ARM) can suddenly and dramatically increase its earnings by bringing a breakthrough product to market, but the annual report in the year before the earnings increase may give no hint of this. The search is on for better ways to measure and report intangibles such as R&D that may have a huge effect on the value of a company.

7. EVA FOR INVESTMENT

As we have seen, EVA is after-tax operating profits minus the appropriate capital charge for both debt and equity. What is so great about it? It is a measure that recognizes that investors must earn enough to compensate for the risk of their investment capital and is a test of whether a firm has "added value" to its shareholders and created wealth in the economy. Use EVA to identify unprofitable activities and potentially valuable acquisitions that other measures fail to show.

8. PERFORMANCE MEASURES

Current management thinking regards performance measurement for executives as a crucial issue. EVA and other measures based on economic profit seem to be defeating competing approaches, such as ROI, because they appear to be more difficult to distort. But is EVA being used to demand managers to excessively over-achieve? The law of averages tells us that, by definition, not all companies can be star performers all of the time. They may nevertheless be good businesses that provide loyal investors with good returns over the long term. Use EVA as a long-term tool, not as electric shock treatment.

9. VALUE ENHANCEMENT – SMALL IMPROVEMENTS

Value is increased by achieving one of these three aims:

1 increasing cash flows from existing investment;
2 creating value-added growth;
3 cutting the cost of capital.

There are very few actions that are pure value creators. In each case there is usually a trade-off with the other factors, and net value will only be created if it outweighs any negative effect. For example, debt payments can be made to match revenues more closely by the use of financial derivatives. If windfall profits from derivatives then come to be seen as an additional objective, the company may take on risks that result in massive losses.

Value can be enhanced by making small improvements in the efficiency of operations, inventory, the tax burden, pricing structure and so on, as detailed in Chapter 6. Taken alone, these improvements may seem insignificant, but the cumulative addition of value can be substantial.

10. VALUE ENHANCEMENT – DEVELOPING MAJOR COMPETITIVE ADVANTAGES

Companies that can create and sustain large competitive advantages are in a position to produce outstanding returns for many years. This is the holy grail of business for many corporations. Competitive advantage implies high barriers to entry – the competition cannot play on a level field. While establishing a world-class brand is the best-known barrier, there are many others. Here are just a few examples.

» Owning natural resources that are easier to extract than those of your competitors.

» Legal protections through government contracts, patents, copyrights, etc.

» Keeping uniquely specialized skills and knowledge within the firm. It is sometimes better not to patent a process, for example, because a patent application makes the invention public. A trade secret may have a much longer life than a patent, especially if it is constantly improved.

» Economies of scale. Some industries, such as airlines and auto manufacturing, are very hard to enter because even if the newcomer has adequate capital, it has difficulty in producing products and services as cheaply as the established players. Such industries tend to be mature, however, so returns may not be above average for long.

KEY POINTS

» Investors and managers have different needs. In a given company, are their interests aligned towards creating value?

» Any estimate of the future is just that, an estimate. No valuation technique provides absolute certainty.

» DCF is probably the best way of valuing a company, but make sure that you fully understand the assumptions on which the calculations are based.

» From the point of view of valuation, the globalization process is a utopian dream. The barriers to capital flows are dropping, allowing investors to move their money across borders but the absence of global accounting standards make it a risky, though potentially rewarding, activity.

» Historical accounting practices are now widely recognized as failing to give adequate information about values. There is a broadly based movement to establish new ways of reporting financial information.

» Some knowledge is valuable, but only if it can be turned into products and services that sell. Intellectual property with legal status, such as patents, are easier to measure because they are definable, but unsubstantiated claims of high value will eventually be tested and a failure to deliver can and does permanently destroy companies and reputations.

» EVA gives you the bottom line: has the company really created wealth? Companies need adequate time in which to do this, so don't abuse EVA by demanding constant quarterly increases. In a recession, these may not be forthcoming.

» Many companies can make numerous small improvements to their efficiency that will significantly enhance value.

» Companies that have major competitive advantages for long periods are likely to create the most value. These are what Warren Buffett likes to call "franchise businesses." While they keep their advantages, they dominate their markets and produce high returns.

NOTES

1 From an article in *Fortune*, "No free lunch: What you don't think about can't hurt you", June 21, 1999, 36.

2 Zarnowitz, V. (1979) "An analysis of analytical and multiperiod quarterly forecasts of aggregate income, output and price level," Journal of Business, 52 (No. 1), 131–46.

Frequently Asked Questions (FAQS)

Q1: What is EVA?

A: See Chapter 2, Economic value added (EVA) and other new proprietary measures.

Q2: What is shareholder value?

A: See Chapter 1.

Q3: How do I calculate NPV and IRR?

A: See Chapter 8, Evaluating investments: discounted cash flow (DCF) and internal rate of return (IRR)

Q4: Why are performance measures so important?

A: See Chapter 2, Economic value added (EVA) and other new proprietary measures and Chapter 8, Are EPPs really better performance measures?

Q5: What is wrong with EPS?

A: See Chapter 2, Earnings per share (EPS) and price/earnings (PE).

Q6: What are real-life examples of high barriers to entry?

A: See Chapter 7, throughout.

Q7: How do you value e-business?

A: See Chapter 4, throughout.

Q8: How do you create value in a business?

A: See Chapter 6, Value enhancement: the financial viewpoint.

Q9: What is wrong with traditional accounting?

A: See Chapter 2, The challenge for senior executives.

Q10: Why do some multinationals pay less tax than others?

A: See Chapter 7, News Corporation.

Index